A Student's Guide to

COPING WITH DEPRESSION

in College

SECOND EDITION

ALSO BY THE AUTHOR

A Professor's Guide to Success in College

Broken Plates & Old Forests

A Student's Guide to

COPING
WITH DEPRESSION

in College

SECOND EDITION

JEFF ANSTINE, PhD

CHICAGO

A STUDENT'S GUIDE TO COPING WITH DEPRESSION IN COLLEGE
SECOND EDITION

First edition published 2020. Second edition published 2024

Windy City Publishers
www.windycitypublishers.com

Printed in the United States of America

ISBN#:
978-1-953294-53-1

Library of Congress Control Number:
2020913414

Front Cover Photo Zmaj88/Shutterstock.com

WINDY CITY PUBLISHERS
CHICAGO

CONTENTS

PREFACE

Wednesday, January 4, 2012, 11:25 a.m.

Oh God no, not now. Not now! I can barely move. It takes all the effort in the world to pick up a pencil and write something. I can barely tap a letter on the computer. Fuck no! Not now!

It's the first day of the winter term. I just spent two hours preparing for classes I'm teaching, two sections of business statistics from 12:00 to 2:30. Then I have a meeting at 3:00, office hours from 4:00 to 6:00 and then my graduate econometrics from 6:30 to 10:30. But I can't do it. It came over me like a tidal wave. My brain barely moves, and my body is paralyzed. This time I really can't.

Fast-forward to 10:45 pm.

I am watching the end of the Orange Bowl, eating a late-night snack. I made it through the day, a long one, working over twelve hours, and nobody knew. They never do. I have been coping with depression for more than forty years. My day was so difficult. But in some ways, it is easier now than it was four decades ago when I was in college.

It gets better, trust me. I could sugarcoat it. Tell you that after you read this book, go to a seminar, see a therapist, or take a drug that everything will be great. It won't, but you already know that. But it will be okay. I don't know when it will be better, and I don't know why it will be better. I just know your depression will improve. And as you get older, you will be able to handle it better.[1]

If I can cope with depression, you can too.[2] I have had episodes of horrible depression since I was about fourteen. One occurrence stands out when I was a sophomore in college. I was so low I didn't feel like attending classes; I skipped some, studied less, and my grades dropped. I was not my "real" self; I avoided people and didn't engage in activities I enjoyed. Nobody understood me—including all my friends—and I dropped out of college.[i]

I wish I knew then what I know now, that overcoming depression is difficult, but life is worth it. Make no mistake, fighting depression is a battle, but the other, better side is always there. It just doesn't seem like it at the time. You can, and will, get through college. You will have spectacular experiences, a rewarding career, and great friends. And if you desire them, a family and many more wonderful things.

---

[1] I will use I, you, and we when describing depression since there are certain unique experiences that only those of us suffering from it know. Just as there are certain things that only people of a particular race, religion, or sexual orientation understand that the rest of us do not. One difference is that we are a largely invisible minority that cuts across all demographics.

[2] I use the word cope very carefully. I don't use cure, fix, solve, or eliminate to describe dealing with the pain. I hope and pray that there is a cure for you. But for many of us there isn't. Nonetheless, there are ways to mitigate the severe pain you feel so you can make it through college and beyond.

INTRODUCTION

It's real common for someone who doesn't have depression to think, "Well, you should just cheer up." And speaking as a person who has had varying degrees of good and bad days, the answer to that is if I could just feel better I would.

~Wil Wheaton
Actor[ii]

A FEW YEARS AGO, THE Provost at Stanford University called mental health "the single highest priority and most compelling need" on its campus.[iii] The Surgeon General has described the mental health of young people in America to be the defining public health crisis of our time.[iv]

I. For Parents, Family, and Others Who Care

High school classes help students get ready for college coursework. As they transition to early adulthood, hopefully they are beginning to handle their finances and other responsibilities. Ideally, they have learned how to cook spaghetti and wash their clothes (ha).

It is better today in many middle and high schools; there are seminars about anxiety, depression, and other mental illnesses. In addition, there are pamphlets, counselors, and other sources of information. However, it is likely that many students are not fully prepared for depression in college.[3]

---

[3] This book is intended to guide students through college. It is not a substitute for professional help from therapists and doctors.

Adolescents often are treated for depression while in high school. In some situations, they (and their parents) think that when they go off to college, the problems that previously existed will go away and they no longer need help. Unfortunately, a new set of stressors can trigger a depressive episode. Students are in a completely different environment, their routines change, and some of their support systems are no longer readily available.

Depression in college students will almost inevitably cause many problems. Young people will have difficulty concentrating, which impacts studying, test taking, and writing papers. An otherwise good student's grades will drop, often significantly to Cs, Ds, and even Fs.

For parents and other people who care, just be sympathetic. If your loved one suffers from depression, they are going through pain that they probably can't describe in a way you can understand. Unlike a broken finger, the flu, mono, or other physical ailments that have obvious symptoms, depression can sometimes be difficult to see. In some cases, there are signs such as not sleeping, sleeping too much, eating disorders, but the connection to depression is sometimes not clear.

Perhaps your child did not talk to you about their depression. If so, it is likely they did not want to reveal their flaws. Or they did not want to disappoint you. You may be angry because you provided so much for them. You may be frustrated because your child is exhibiting unusual behavior. Depression can make us forgetful, irritable, and afraid. It's likely your child will also have very low energy, so it may appear that they are lazy.

As a parent, you might also feel guilty. We want our children to be happy, well-adjusted individuals. For some of us, if our children are less than perfect, we feel it makes us look bad as parents. You might be sad because you feel your child's pain. Or you may feel helpless because you are unable to fix it. But there are some steps you can take during their time of need.

First, don't blame yourself or them. This is something that is out of your or their control. Realize that you are not alone! In one of many recent studies, 45% of college students reported symptoms of depression.[v] The number of college students with depression is probably higher, since there are many young people who do not seek help or are not diagnosed.

Second, be careful what you say. You want to provide support so you may think that words of encouragement will help. It may, however, do just the opposite. Don't say: "Look on the bright side." (They can't.) "You are lucky." (They know that.) "It could be worse." (That may be true, but it is difficult for them to see it.) "Snap out of it." (It is not possible.)

It is difficult for people suffering from depression to move toward those who do not. You need to figure out how to go where they are. Broad comments are best. For example, "How can I help?" "What are you feeling?" "How do you hurt?" But realize that you might not be able to "fix" it.

Third, let your loved one know that you are on their side. Tell them that you will help guide them but don't force them to say or do anything. When they talk to you, be sure to listen, nonjudgmentally. Empathize the same way you would if they had a physical ailment. Do not trivialize the way they are feeling.

If you are going to discuss your loved one's depression with other people, be careful who you share it with. If you are going to contact people at the college, start with the associate dean of students or whomever is in charge of student affairs. They can relay information to professors, resident assistants, dorm-mates, and other people connected to your child.

If you have friends or family you trust, share your concerns with them. If you think that others would not understand, you are under no obligation to say anything. If someone asks, just say "my child/son/daughter is feeling low or out of sorts."

II. For Students

Getting depression at any time is horrible. Having it during college has other implications too. This is a time when you are moving into adulthood, developing a sense of who you are and where you fit in the world. While depression can complicate this, it does not stop your growth into a full, healthy, well-rounded individual.

If someone has given you this book, it shows that they care about you. While this will not cure your depression, it is one of dozens of reasons to move forward with your life. Get help from others while also doing as much as you can yourself.

If you got this book for yourself, without the knowledge of parents or others, you may be hiding your depression from them. You may be doing this for a variety of reasons. One is that you feel bad and do not want to hurt your family or you want to protect them. This is natural and if you can share with them, you should. Trust yourself; however, if you really feel that they are unable or unwilling to help, sharing will only place an additional burden on you.

Another reason you might not want to share your experiences is that you are from a family that will not accept it. There may be a history of abuse, neglect, or alcoholism that make your family not supportive or unwilling to help you. Or some people in your family have mental illness themselves but are incapable of acknowledging problems like depression. If this is the case, I am very sorry; trust me, I know how difficult this is. The good news is that if you have made it this far without support, you have proven that you have the inner strength to make it further through college on your own. You are smart enough to recognize you need guidance and this book will direct you through what you need to do.

III. For Both Students and Others Who Care

There are different levels of depression and the amount of help available will vary depending on the level of severity. If you or someone you know is having suicidal thoughts, sending signs of hurting themselves or others, call 988 for the National Suicide and Crisis Lifeline (https://988lifeline.org/).[4] Or text HOME to 741741 to connect with a volunteer crisis counselor.

For those of you who care for someone with depression, at first provide as much help as possible, but in the future (weeks, months, or years), be sure that you do not overly enable them. As parents, sometimes we help our children so much that we inadvertently do more harm than good. Some parents have been so supportive handling their child's depression that the student has difficulty handling daily chores by themselves.

This book is intended to guide you through your college career with help on classes, advising, and other academic items. While I do provide some advice on therapy, I do not go into detail on pharmacology, psychological jargon, or other medical information. As a professor of quantitative business and environmental management, I am far from an expert on these areas.

However, I am uniquely qualified to write this book. I attended two universities as an undergraduate and another as a graduate student, hitting bouts of depression in each. I had a successful career in the private sector for about five years in my twenties before returning to get my Ph.D. I have taught three dozen different classes at five colleges and universities. In addition, I have

---

[4] You can call 988 just like you can call 911 directly in case of an emergency. This is a step forward in acknowledging that mental illness is a serious problem in society.

taught classes in other countries. I have worked with undergraduate students from their first class on campus to taking graduate students to Costa Rica for a class on local business conditions. I have advised students on classes they should take, have overseen internships, and served in practically every role as a college professor.

This book is for college students suffering from depression and can be read in a few hours. It is short because when somebody is depressed, they do not have the energy to read a long, complicated work. Note that it would be helpful to have another person read it with the student to help implement the steps needed to succeed in college while combating this disease.

This book is primarily aimed at the traditional college experience of taking classes in person. However, it is still very relevant in the post-pandemic, now endemic era with some changes in classes. For example, the information on how to pick classes and still fill general education requirements to graduate on time holds for online and hybrid courses too.

Again, a disclaimer: This book is not a replacement for help from professional mental health care experts.

I KNOW YOUR PAIN

What's wrong with me? Why am I the only person going through this? I was in a big hole. I started getting depressed because I thought I was losing control of everything.

~Kyle Wilson
Former college basketball player[vi]

I AM SO SORRY. I don't know you. Nobody truly understands the agony you feel. But if you are suffering from depression, I know your pain as much as anybody. Life is extremely difficult for you right now. It is possibly worse than any physical pain you have ever had. It is an enormous struggle to move. Getting out of bed seems impossible. Walking takes all the effort in the world.

Psychiatrists and health care professionals define a major depressive disorder as five or more of the following symptoms present for two weeks:

- Depressed mood most of the day
- Irritability
- Decreased interest or pleasure in most activities
- Significant change in weight or appetite
- Change in sleep
- Increased agitation or sluggishness
- Fatigue or loss of energy
- Feelings of guilt or worthlessness
- Changes in concentration and recurrent thoughts of death[5]

---

[5] There are also other definitions of depression that include Seasonal Affective Disorder (SAD).

The official definition may be useful to some people, but it might not completely describe you; it doesn't for me. My depression is more complex than this and yours likely is too. When I am low or melancholy, the sensations are bearable and okay. However, these are very different from the feelings I experience with depression, which is horrendous and overwhelming.

In other situations, depression is defined as self-loathing or a lack of self-esteem. Again, this does not fit me because even when I am lower than low, I hold myself in high regard and do not hate myself.

There are hundreds, perhaps thousands, of types of depression. If you suffer from severe depression, you are in a group that someone who has not gone through it could never understand. Below are some possible explanations for you, and maybe others who care.

1. Horrendous emotional and often physical pain

All the pain in the world is concentrated in your body and mind. I was diagnosed with prostate cancer when I was fifty. After I woke up from the surgery to remove it, before receiving any pain medication, I was in excruciating agony. I had six deep cuts in my belly, pain from having part of my insides cut out, and distress from seeing blood dripping from holes in my body and private parts.

There was the visible suffering that others could see and the invisible fear that only I felt. The psychological pain of the invisible was worse than the horrible physical pain. I feared that the cancer had spread throughout my body. I dreaded that I would be infirm, getting weaker each month until I died a few years later. I felt horrible distress that I would not see my young children grow up.[6]

My pain from depression has been as bad.[7] The pain can be overwhelming but is invisible and impossible to describe or make comparisons. One question I hate is when medical clinicians ask, "On a scale of one to ten, how high is your pain?" They asked this after I came out of anesthesia. I hurt like hell—that's it. If

---

[6] I did delay writing this book because, after my battle with cancer, I did (not surprisingly) have another bout of depression that lasted for a long period of time.

[7] I am NOT minimizing the agony that cancer causes. Other types of cancer are worse than mine and childhood cancer is horrendous. I am just trying to explain how much depression hurts physically in addition to emotionally. Which is worse, depression or cancer? It is impossible to answer. Did my suffering from depression help or hurt in my battle with cancer? I don't know. Both are just horrible.

you stabbed me with the scalpel you just used to slice me open, I would prob-ably hurt more but *I simply just HURT.* It is the same with your depression, you are in agony. There is a huge weight on you so that you can barely breathe. Your head is splitting with the worst migraine. Your body aches and muscles tremble as from a horrible flu.

When I was diagnosed with cancer and then later as I was recovering, some acquaintances said, "You look good." It was probably well-intentioned, but the comments really hurt. I wanted to reply, "F-YOU, I look good, I feel like crap!"

You may have had people say the same thing to you about your depression. "You look fine." Or, "It doesn't look like there is anything wrong with you." And you probably wanted to respond, "Maybe I look fine, but I am going through hell!"

2. Frustration

You may be frustrated because nobody understands you. Some people may confuse your depression with laziness or a lack of moral fortitude. From the outside, another person sees a lack of motivation. You know that this is not the real you. You are used to functioning on a high level but now you are not capable of it. While other people may lack awareness of what you feel, it does not mean that they are incapable of compassion.

3. Guilt

You might feel guilty because you are not the same son/daughter/child for your parents. You do not do as much for your girlfriend/boyfriend/partner. You are not as supportive of your friends. I have been on the other side. When I was severely depressed, I was not as good of a parent to my kids. I can admit this because I know that overall I have been a very good dad. Just as I am sure that you have been a great person to all your close ones.

4. Down deep

All lows are not the same; some are related to depression while others are not. For example, there is the low energy you feel when you are tired from working hard on a job, class work, or a physical activity. You may be tired, but you feel good because you accomplished something.

There is also the low energy that doesn't feel good due to insomnia or not eating well and not exercising. Going about life is harder than normal, but it isn't horrible either. And there is a low that can feel good. You are melancholy, and may reflect on life, thinking about the bad—and the good.

Then, of course, there is the hellish depression low when you have almost no energy at all. In the depression low, you can't tell how down you are. If it is 15 degrees below zero one day and 17 degrees below the next day, it is just freezing. When you are severely low, you can't compare one depression to another. You are on the bottom of the ocean where there is no light, you are suffocating and cannot move.

5. Scared

When your unwanted companion arrives, it often brings other demons with it. You are afraid but do not know why. You have no control over your thoughts, feelings, and emotions. You feel something bad may happen, though you have no idea what it would even be. You are insecure making simple decisions.

6. Lonely

You may be surrounded by friends, walking with classmates across campus, going into your dorm with other students playing Ping-Pong. It makes no sense, but you feel all alone. Hopefully you have a mom, dad, brother, sister, or other relative who truly and honestly loves you. But they cannot fix or cure you. (If you do not have anybody, you can still make it.)

7. Slower

Somebody makes a joke that you did not get. You didn't understand something simple someone said and are confused. It takes more concentration to listen to others and pay attention. Your brain is moving at half speed. You are embarrassed because you are usually smart and witty. You are disappointed that your mind is not working the way it should. The real/other you can tackle any problem, make friends, is social and friendly. The depressed you is not.

8. Physically weak

When I am feeling fine, I can lift light weights, jog, exercise, and move without too much effort. When I am depressed, I can't lift the same amount, I run slower, and am sometimes clumsy. When you are depressed, you do not have the strength you normally do to go about your typical routine.

9. Not (necessarily) sad!

For me there is a huge difference between being really sad and being depressed. Sad is when your boyfriend breaks up with you. Sad is the death of a close relative. Sad is when koala bears die in wildfires in Australia. There are many things in life that make us sad, and some of these can also trigger depression, but they can also be different.

VERY SAD

VERY HAPPY

Sometimes depression is defined as chronic sadness. For me, depression is not with this scale of sadness. You may have depression-like symptoms that are similar to sadness, but they may also be very different. There are lots of things that make me sad, but my depression is a very different feeling. In the summer of 2020 I was not only depressed but also had long-Covid, problems breathing, fatigue, and had a mental breakdown. I was extremely sad when my now ex-wife told me she wanted a divorce. I was both depressed AND very sad.[8]

10. Unstable

I am afraid to admit how unstable I feel occasionally when I am depressed. It is not a feeling that I am going to hurt anyone else or do anything illegal or unethical. I just do not feel as if I am connected to the world.

---

[8] Sad is in some ways a stronger sensation. It hits you in a more immediate way. It is almost always triggered by an event, external or personal. Sadness can last a day, week, month, or more. Depression can occur at any time without any particular reason.

11. Death-like

Maybe it is not feelings of suicide, but you do not feel like living. Nothing gives you pleasure or hope. If you think about death, do not go down that path. The world is a better place with you; you are a wonderful person who is going to do great things. If you are having suicidal thoughts call 988 for the National Suicide and Crisis Lifeline https://988lifeline.org/. Or text HOME to 741741 to connect with a volunteer crisis counselor.

12. Anxiety

With your depression, you may also experience anxiety. I find that I am more anxious when depressed, so that when I cope with my depression, it also alleviates this problem. When I find myself worrying about unreasonable things, I try to put on my "logical" side to minimize the anxiety.

13. Other mental illnesses

I hope it is not the case, but in addition to depression, you may experience other mental health disorders. If you suffer from things like obsessive-compulsive behavior, be sure to get these treated too.[9]

Just because other people do not know what you are experiencing, it does not mean that your depression is not real. In the next chapter, I provide a few examples of how depression in college may hit you.

14. Missing words

It is impossible to accurately describe your depression. Part of the problem with depression is that there are not strong enough words for it. There are cancer survivors, which is an appropriate term, as it can be a life and death situation. There are auto accident victims who have had to fight through rehabilitation. In the thousands of pages that I have read about depression I have yet to see an accurate description for my depression; perhaps you have one. **It may help you to put into words what you are feeling in order to make the abstract nature of your depression more concrete.**

---

[9] If you are experiencing significant mood disorders other than depression, be sure and get treatment. This book focuses on depression so is outside the scope of other psychological problems.

WHEN, HOW, AND WHY DEPRESSION HITS

I would describe it as I'd be sitting there having a conversation.
Everything would be fine and then I would just be in tears.
It's knowing the pain, you know, how just awful it is.

~Dorothy Hamill
Olympic gold medalist[vii]

1. When It Hits

- Midnight talking to your friend in your dorm room in the third week of the first semester of your sophomore year.

- 9:15 am in the overheated classroom during a lecture on U.S. government in the fifth week of your second semester during your first year.

- Noon eating mediocre food by yourself in the dining hall during finals week in your first semester.

- 10:24 pm in the library studying for your philosophy midterm exam.

- 1:42 pm during your first calculus test.

You get the idea.

2. How It Hits

Your depression may hit in a variety of ways. You may gradually go from being yourself to slowing sinking lower, until you can barely move.

Sometimes it just hits. You are fine, and then, suddenly, it knocks you out like a bolt of lightning. There is no warning. You go to sleep at night feeling fine and wake up the next day (or in the middle of the night) feeling horrible.

Or you may oscillate, up and down. You feel fine one hour then low the next. You are a yo-yo, going up, down, up, down, up, down until the string snaps and you fall into depression.

Perhaps it hits in a way that only you experience. There are a million permutations of this disease with each of us in our own unique hell each time it occurs.

3. Why It Hits

It is likely that you are genetically predisposed to depression. There is some combination of environmental or social factors and inherited characteristics that trigger it. Just an unlucky mix that causes it at some point with no foreseeable reason. Or your depression may be triggered by an event. An aunt's cancer diagnosis, a grandfather's death, or your parents' divorce. It may have been a response to a national emergency, such as the outbreak of Covid-19. Possibly the pandemic worsened your depression from mild to severe.

Your depression could have been caused by discrimination based on the color of your skin, sexual orientation, appearance, or other characteristic. It may be due to bullying, being excluded from social groups or something from social media.

It may hit in your first year. The freedom and uncertainty associated with college can be a little scary. You may be away from home, parents, friends, and familiar surroundings. You could feel intimidated or alone.

You may be homesick. You have spent eighteen years with your family, friends, and neighbors. You have developed a routine that is very predictable. Movies with your friends on Friday nights, lunch with your boyfriend every Thursday, pasta for dinner every Monday, Sunday watching football with your dad.

Depression could occur during your sophomore year. The initial excitement and novelty of college has worn off. Then the stress of coursework, a job, and extracurricular activities may be overwhelming.

It may occur in your junior year. The first two years have been filled with making friends, joining clubs, getting used to the college routine, and finding your niche. Now that you have established yourself and are comfortable in your environment, depression hits.

Maybe it happens when you are a senior, close to graduation. You are anxious about the future or there is uncertainty about jobs. Your living arrangements are likely changing, your career will be starting soon, and the true beginning of adulthood is upon you.

It may hit because of change. Many major changes in life patterns are good: graduating from high school, getting married, having children, getting promoted at work. However, even good change is stressful, and the change from high school to college, with more responsibility, can be a huge challenge.

It may just be growing up. Your mind and body are still shifting. You have yet to completely develop into an adult. Your body image, feelings, and emotions are still in the process of maturing.

Perhaps depression occurs because you learned about something in a class that triggered it. Some research has shown that knowledge of climate disruption leading to drastic changes in the world, genocide of a countries' citizens, or other troubling topics can exacerbate emotions.

It could be related to the seasons. Daylight has a positive impact on our moods. When it gets darker earlier during the winter we are exposed to less sun, which can lead to depression. Even the daylight savings time change is enough for depression to occur in some people.

It is very possible that you don't know why it happens. Your depression may be random; the way a tornado picks a certain house to demolish and leaves the home next door completely intact.

I will provide more information on how to cope with depression during your life at the end of Chapter 7. The next chapter describes situations of some students who have struggled with depression, overcome it, graduated, and went on to future success.

EXAMPLES OF STUDENTS COPING WITH DEPRESSION, OVERCOMING IT, AND GRADUATING

I know how alone I felt and how sad I felt.

~Chamique Holdsclaw
Three-time NCAA basketball champion and WNBA player[viii]

WHILE TEACHING AT FIVE COLLEGES and universities, I have directly seen dozens of students suffering from depression. I have witnessed signs of depression in hundreds of others. I am sure there are hundreds more that have been in my classes where I was completely unaware of their pain. I've seen depression happen to a student as it hits them over a week. In others, I have witnessed it during the course of a month and in others, over a few years.

In the past, with the majority of students, I tried to send a subtle hint for them to hang in there. Usually generically for the entire class. I made up an example, illustrating course material that I incorporated into my lecture. For most students, it is just another way to learn about management or statistics. For the depressed students, I hope that they got the hidden meaning embedded in my examples; that I want them to be okay.

On occasion, I wrote a comment on a paper or test when I returned it, encouraging them to push ahead. When appropriate, I sent an email expressing my concerns. In my experience, I think some students appreciated it while most probably didn't even recognize it.

A number of students from my classes or other roles, such as an advisor, approach me. It usually starts with them saying they were disappointed about a test grade or other academic problem. As we talk, it becomes clear that there is a deeper issue beyond college coursework. These students are fraught with anxiety, struggling with their sexuality, a relationship, or other personal problems. In many situations, students are suffering from depression.

With students who admit they are depressed, after listening to them, I reveal that I have struggled with it too. Without going into detail, I give them words of encouragement and then talk about strategies for improving in class (I go into detail on that in the next couple of chapters). I make it clear that I am sympathetic but refer them to the health center to see a counselor emphasizing that I am not a therapist.

I have had a significant number of students email me about their struggles with depression. I reply that I am very sorry, that I understand. Then tell them to be sure to get help and wish them well.

I am certain there have been hundreds of other students with depression where I was not helpful. All I saw was poor attendance, laziness, rude behavior, not any underlying problems with mental health.

I used to be more helpful in the past. Today, most of the time I don't do anything because I am overwhelmed with students with mental illness. My first and primary responsibility is as a professor, and I always fulfill my obligations there. However, I do briefly address depression and other ailments at the beginning of my classes. In my syllabus I have a statement that discusses mental health indirectly.

Statement from your Professor:

I know that life can be challenging sometimes and at other times extremely difficult. (Trust me, I know better than anyone.) I hope that you go through life and college smoothly, but I know that there are lots of problems and complications. While I do care about you as a person, my first priority is as your professor.

On the positive side I have witnessed many students with depression be successful. Below are a few examples of some who have struggled with depression in college, managed to make it through, graduate, and move on to professional careers.[10]

1. Sophomore Female Vice President of Student Group

I had one young woman in a management class in a fall term. She was friendly, intelligent, hardworking, and did well on all the assignments. I chatted with her occasionally after class and got to know her a little. She was involved in a few student groups, had an active social life, and seemed to be a typical college sophomore. She finished the class with a solid A.

The following winter term I had her in a statistics class. I enjoy having students I know from previous classes because we have already developed a faculty-student relationship. This familiarity often helps me establish a rapport with the other students and sets the tone for a respectful, productive class.

On Monday during the fourth week, she was in class, on time, as always. However, on Wednesday she was late for class and not prepared. When she walked into class on Friday, I could see the aura of depression surrounding her. Her face was sullen; her body movements were slow and deliberate. Her notes were disorganized, and she was struggling to pay attention.

The next week, she missed a class of mine for the first time. She continued being late and would leave immediately after it, not talking to other students like she typically did. After I returned the second test, she stayed after class to talk to me. She got a C-, a big drop from all her other assignments.

---

[10] These are composites of students and details have been changed so that specific people cannot be identified.

She told me she was disappointed in her performance. She did poorly because she was having difficulty concentrating (which is the same thing that happens to me when I hit a depressive episode) and that was why she had made mistakes.

I told her I empathized, that I knew she was smart and hard-working, that this was a temporary aberration, and that she would do better in the future. Without directly telling her, I tried to convey that I knew where her problems stemmed from and that she would be okay, encouraging her to keep going.

She struggled to manage her depression but continued with the class; working as hard as she could, did well on the remaining assignments and finished with a decent grade. She asked me for a recommendation for studying abroad. I wrote her a letter and filled out the generic form. One question on it asks if you (I) have any concerns about the student. It was very difficult for me to do and made me think about depression and student opportunities more. I was very concerned about her depression, but also worried that if I mentioned it, she might not be accepted. I strongly feel that those of us with depression should not be discriminated against. So, I said I no, I had no concerns.

She spent four months studying in Europe, did great in the program, and traveled while there. I was happy to see that depression did not keep her from a life-changing experience. After she returned to the United States, she continued with her activities and graduated with honors. The last I knew she had a good job and was succeeding in life.

2. Senior Male Football Player

Years ago, I had an athlete in one of my classes as a first-year student, and then again as a sophomore; he did very well in both courses. He was a big, strong guy but also polite and a hard worker. I saw him at a few games and around campus occasionally. We greeted each other and I would complement him on his game if he had played well or ask about upcoming opponents.

After a year, he drifted away, as most of my students do, going on with their classes and activities. Then at the beginning of his senior year, he emailed me to ask if I would be his academic advisor since he had changed majors. I replied telling him I would be happy to and told him to stop by my office so that we could set up his classes and make sure he graduated on time.

When I got access to his academic files, I had a strong suspicion of what happened. The A's and Bs he got his first two years had dropped to Cs, Ds, and an F in his junior year. He had not even signed up for classes for the upcoming term. When I met with him, I asked how his team was doing. He told me he had also stopped playing football. I asked why, knowing the likely answer. He responded that he had just lost interest in it as he had with other college activities. My suspicion was confirmed; his behavior exhibited clear signs of depression.

He was late registering, so I helped him put his schedule together. I got him in the required courses, and we developed an academic plan for getting him through to graduation. Then our conversation moved back to his low grades the previous year. He was worried that this might limit his future opportunities.

Being careful with my words, I told him about my struggles in college and some poor grades when I was an undergraduate student due my "low" periods. I told him that this might set him back a little, but it was a temporary blip on his way to a successful future. I felt awkward consoling a six-foot-four guy who was 245 pounds of muscle. But I felt even worse for his pain.

Depression does not discriminate. On the surface, he is strong, likeable, smart, and attractive. I imagine this made it even worse for him. These guys are not allowed to be weak and when you are depressed, you are weak in so many ways. The good news was his grades went up and he finished his undergraduate studies. The last I knew he was in graduate school doing very well.

3. Shy, Studious Female Junior

In an international business course of forty students, three weeks into the class, a woman approached me after a lecture. I appreciate this because in larger classes it is more difficult for me to get to know students. When they reach out, I get to know them a little. She really liked an example I used about Eastern Europe, where her family was from. We talked for a while about the culture and history of her home country and then about the upcoming test.

She did well on the exam. However, over the following weeks she attended class sporadically and then failed the second test. She didn't show up to class the following week, so I emailed asking if she was okay, but knowing she probably was not. She replied, confirming it, saying that she was suffering from depression but was getting help.

I replied saying I was glad she was seeking treatment and that her health was the most important thing; but to hang in there, that she could still make it through not just my class but also through school. She got her depression under control, was able to complete all the assignments and managed to finish the class with a C+. Two years later, I was happy when I saw her walk across the stage getting her diploma.

4. Typical Guy Student

I had known one former student for well over a decade. He was typical of the male sophomores in my introductory business classes. Slightly overweight, not disinterested in the class but also not one of the more serious students. He wore his baseball cap backwards and sat in the back row. He was talking with his buddies about the Bears when I returned his first test with a B- on it.

I was surprised when he stopped by my office about halfway through the term since he was doing fine (such students tend to avoid much direct contact with professors). We talked a little about the class, but it was clear he had other things on his mind. After he felt comfortable, he brought up other non-academic problems he was going through, being moderately depressed but still able to function.

I told him that I empathized with his difficult situation, but that he still needed to focus on college. He already knew that, but just needed to hear it from someone else. I continued to talk with him occasionally throughout his college career. The last I knew he was a successful executive, happy in his job, making more money than I do. We had lunch together every couple of years until he took a promotion in another city.

I have used these stories to illustrate what separates students with depression who succeed and those who do not. **All these students handled their depression in a mature manner. They did not blame other people for their problems and took responsibility for their coursework.**

It is likely there were other situations where I was not helpful. A student in one of my classes may have been doing poorly due to depression and I was not or did not seem helpful. My job is to ensure that I teach my classes in a rigorous but fair manner. If students are not showing up to class and/or spend their time on their electronic devices instead of paying attention and do not do the required work I assume that they are not college material.

I have had some students approach me and talk about their depression. I told them I was very sorry. However, these students who did not succeed were also inconsiderate of other students, rude, or self-centered. These are unrelated to depression. It was these characteristics that caused their failure. They would disrupt class or tell me that I just had to give them a good grade because of their problems. They ended up failing due to a lack of work and blamed me. There is a huge difference between having low energy due to depression and being lazy, not taking responsibility for class work.

At most colleges and universities, over the past decade, there has been pressure for professors to put more information on their syllabi and in their classes on subjects unrelated to the class. This includes material on LBGTQIA and other groups, including people with mental health issues. This is good, but a calculus professor still needs to teach derivatives and integrals. As a student, keep in mind that learning the material, critical thinking, and other academic items are the main point of the class. So, there may be some support, but it is best not to expect it.

My biggest piece of advice for college students with depression is to be careful. Be cautious about telling professors. If they reach out to you it is because they care, and it is okay to talk. Don't over-share, save that for a qualified professional. But know that many of us are on your side and want you to be not just okay mentally but successful as well. And though you may feel very alone and hopeless, you can, and will, improve as you go through college, graduate, and on to a rewarding life.

STIGMA, GUILT, OBSTACLES, AND DEMONS

Our society frowns on it (depression).
And they (society) don't want their heroes to have these issues.
How can you be depressed, you're such a funny guy.
But depression doesn't rob you of your personality.

~Terry Bradshaw
NFL Hall of Fame quarterback and football commentator[ix]

UNFORTUNATELY, STRUGGLES WITH DEPRESSION ARE not isolated to just the pain of it; there are other unwanted side effects that make it even more difficult.

1. Stigma

As a college student, you may have hidden your depression from other students, friends, faculty, and others. You have very valid reasons for this. Your sorority only wants happy, perky members. Your baseball coach thinks it is a sign that you are weak and won't play you. The study abroad advisor thinks you will be incapable of living with a host family. Your roommate thinks you will cause problems. Your friends don't want to hang out with an unsocial person.

Some people think that if you suffer from depression it will inhibit your ability to engage in certain activities. Or that you will need special accommodations. Or you will pose a risk of some sort. Society has many misconceptions about depression. This holds true even with young people in institutions of

24

higher education. In a study of 62,171 college students, 47% of them agree with the statement, "Most people would think less of someone who has received mental health treatment."[x]

In my twenties, I was afraid of admitting my depression to friends because I thought I might lose them. If I admitted it in my thirties, I was fearful of repercussions from my employers. In my forties, I was afraid to talk about it because it might scare my wife and embarrass my kids. Even today, with tenure, job security, and a more than four-decade record of hard work and responsibility, I am still nervous about "coming out." Not to mention the "guys are supposed to be strong" mentality.

Nonetheless, while you do not necessarily want to broadcast your struggles with depression, you should find the right people and outlets to help you with it. I will cover this in upcoming chapters.

We are a long way from being a society with an open mind, but we have made progress in some areas over the past few decades. With many steps backwards, we have become a little more open to people of different races, sexuality, and other differences. In the 2020s, is it okay to identify oneself as somewhat mentally ill with depression? I am not sure that it is-there is still a huge stigma associated with it. It follows then, that there is a fear of acknowledging it to others.

2. Guilt

Associated with the stigma is guilt. The guilt you feel from having depression only exacerbates the problem. You are disappointing your dad. It makes your mom sad. You do not want to make your parents look bad and you may need to "keep up appearances" for a variety of reasons. You may be fortunate in many ways, so other people think you shouldn't feel so low.

It is a disease and one that more adolescents are dealing with every year. In a study from 2023, 44% of students reported symptoms of depression and 37% reported anxiety.[xi] Though it may help to know that many other people suffer from it, in some ways it does not matter because you are not just a statistic! Because there is not a Misericordia, Relay for Life, or other large organization raising money for awareness of the problem does not mean it is any less important.[xii]

Do not feel guilty about your depression *because it is not your fault.* There are an increasing number of movies, plays, books, and art exhibits that are shedding light on depression. Not to mention the increasing number of athletes, actors, musicians, and other people revealing their struggles. In the future, there will likely be more acceptance of this disease.

3. Obstacles

Colleges and universities are typically open, welcoming, accepting institutions. There are hundreds of friendly staff, faculty, and students who are willing to help you with almost any problem. There are offices to help students with learning disabilities. There are support groups for the LGBTQIA community. There are policies to accommodate people with peanut allergies. And there are services to help students in distress.

However, depressed students sometimes have more hurdles and fewer resources than others. Colleges have (justified) reasons for not wanting any negative publicity and for avoiding any potential problems that could occur due to a student's behavior. Colleges have policies, both written and unwritten, to help protect themselves from homicidal and suicidal individuals.

The lawsuits and negative publicity from a student seriously harming themselves or others is one of the larger worries that college administrators have. Though people with depression are extremely unlikely to cause serious harm, misperceptions may make administrators overreact. In addition, there may not be enough resources (staff, money, time) to adequately address mental health problems.

There have been circumstances in the past where students have had difficulties with their school after exhibiting certain behaviors. A student at George Washington University was forbidden from entering his dorm after taking many pills and ending up in the hospital. A student at Hunter College was also locked out of her dorm after swallowing lots of Tylenol and calling 911.[xiii]

Today, there are more students with mental illness attending college than ever before. The vast majority of students do not pose a problem for themselves or others. Colleges are trying to balance the psychological health needs of students with legal, financial, privacy, and other concerns.

Thus, colleges do have involuntary withdrawal policies where, if a staff or faculty member believes a student could cause harm to themselves, others, or to property, the student can be forced to leave. Nonetheless, there are people to help you. (There is more on this in Chapter 5.)

4. Demons (or Some Other Invisible Ailment)

Nobody is perfect and everybody has some kind of inner turmoil. Some people are lucky. They have annoying feelings that appear from time to time. These little devils make them prickly and unpleasant for a day or two. But they are small and insignificant and thus are shooed away like a fly and disappears quickly.

Other people have problems they don't even know exist. Some individuals stumble through life, failing in school and jobs, moving from one dysfunctional relationship to another. They never even acknowledge, let alone face and come to grips with, the insecurities responsible for their difficulties.

For some of us, when we are depressed, we are in our own private hell with invisible beasts attacking us. The monster that hit you yesterday is different from the ogre that is eating at your insides today. Sometimes the demon is so strong it immobilizes you, sucking all your energy.

I do not know your specific demons, but I do know mine. After graduating from college in my early twenties, I lived in New York City. In my early thirties, I lived in Newark, New Jersey. To try to fight the demons caused by my depression during those times, I sought out the worst parts of those cities. I felt so low that the only place I felt at home was where buildings were literally falling down.

I walked around areas filled with junkies, drug dealers, and prostitutes. People injecting needles, shivering from withdrawal, nodding off from their last hit. The saddest of the sad, people in enormous pain. They would stare at me as I walked through the slums. Sometimes they would yell an insult or two, but usually not. They could tell that there was clearly something wrong with me. I wandered around staring at them; it seemed that they were the only people in the world who shared my despair. Find an outlet for your demons, but do not do something reckless and dangerous like I did.

You may be engaged in actions of self-harm. You may be cutting yourself with razors or burning yourself with cigarettes or a lighter. Maybe you engage in risky sexual behavior. Perhaps you drive recklessly while intoxicated. You can manage this pain unlike your lack of control over your mental pain. **There are many ways depressed individuals try to mask their pain. If you are doing something that is self-destructive, please get help immediately.** Again, be sure the help is from a qualified professional, since this is often misunderstood by most of society. There can be the misperception that self-harm is a suicide attempt.

5

DEALING WITH DEPRESSION IN THE SHORT TERM (HOURS TO DAYS TO A FEW WEEKS)

I didn't really realize what was going on.
I remember just being stuck in the house and trying to
do things to make myself happy, and I couldn't.

~Ricky Williams
Heisman Trophy running back[xiv]

DEPRESSION IS ONE OF THE most debilitating conditions a college student can face. Whether it is mild or severe, depression impedes success. When it hits, here are things you can do in the short term, to make sure you get through your classes.

1. Coping Immediately

You are in pain! It is okay to feel it. Don't deny it. Cry, scream, run, let it out. Listen to your favorite music. Don't try to fight it. It is like a riptide in an ocean current. If you swim directly against it, it will pull you even farther out in the ocean. If you swim away along the shoreline, you can avoid its pull, and then swim safely into the shore.

Take time for you. Take a long, hot shower. Indulge in your favorite TV show. Catch up on the gossip on your preferred website. Watch the silly YouTube or TikTok videos. Binge on that Netflix series. Take a long walk (research has shown that walking helps clear your mind and can alleviate depression). Pet a cat. Do this just enough to rebalance, but don't get caught in a hole where you do this for weeks on end.

Listen to and trust yourself. If you suffer from depression, you know it. You don't have to take an online quiz. You don't need a person asking you to rate how sad you are on a scale from one to ten. You may have to hide it from other people but don't deny it to yourself.

2. Get Help from Your High School Therapist or from the Counseling Center

If you have gotten help from a therapist or other individual that you are not seeing now, contact them immediately to get help again. If you are not living close to them, set up a phone call, Zoom, or another virtual visit if possible. The following information is for students who are experiencing their first bout of depression or have not sought help for it in the past.

You may have gotten some emotional support from another student, a coach, staff, or professor. It is likely that you need more care. Almost all colleges have some kind of counseling service to help you. **On your school's website go to the tab for current students. The information you need will be under either student services or academic support services.** There will be something about health services and then under that, information on the college's mental health provision.

The health service center has social workers or psychologists who can talk to you when you are feeling very low or if you just need somebody to listen. Most schools in the U.S. have become much more proactive in letting students know about the resources available for mental health services. If you can't find it, go directly to the student health center in person.

Seek help as soon as you can. It may take a few hours or days to see someone, so set up an appointment immediately. Using resources and asking for assistance is often the hardest part. Many people think that it is a sign of weakness to admit a problem; however, it is just the opposite. It shows maturity and strength to admit when we need help. If you are too low to do it yourself, ask for help from your dorm supervisor, orientation leader, first year mentors, campus security, a roommate, or anyone close. You do not need to tell them why you need the appointment if you do not want to.

Depending on their size, commitment to students' mental health, location, and other factors, different schools have diverse approaches to helping with depression. No matter what services your school offers, be forceful (while polite) in making sure you get help. Your student fees are paying for this. Be aware that the demand for all support services by students has increased dramatically, so it may be difficult to get an appointment. If you are experiencing significant problems, emphasize this to ensure you are made a priority. Here are some things you may encounter.

In general, there are three screening methods for college students before referring them for help. One is a phone interview where a counselor will ask questions to determine the severity of your problems and what the appropriate treatment is. The second is similar: You will talk with someone from the health center—in person—to determine what the next step is. Third, you may have to fill out a questionnaire on the website and then will be contacted about what to do next. Go directly to the health center and ask for help in person if navigating the system through the website or phone is too complex. When you do meet with someone for help, you will likely be required to sign a confidentiality agreement.

The type of treatment and length of time it lasts varies drastically by schools, from just a peripheral visit with a counselor to more thorough treatment. Here are some possibilities: One, you will see a licensed professional who can help you for enough sessions that will get you back on track with your life. Two, you will see a temporary counselor who will see you for a few sessions as they help set you up with a more permanent treatment plan outside the school.

Three, you will meet with someone one time and they will refer you to potential treatment options on campus. These include meeting with graduate students who are training for a profession in the mental health area. These individuals may counsel you for a longer period of time. Or you may also be referred to a support group with other students that are led by a qualified therapist. Some colleges are increasingly using peer counseling where other undergraduate students provide support for other undergraduate students who are struggling with their mental health.

Technology is increasingly used to supplement or replace parts of the process. You may be given videos to watch online. A counselor may then help you and give other assignments online to treat you. In addition, there are also interactive games that are intended to alleviate your symptoms.

In some cases, counselors at the health centers work with other staff to take a multifaceted approach to treatment. You may be referred to a "wellness" coach who will help with time management, stress reduction, diet, and exercise that will help alleviate some of your depression.

If you are working with a therapist for a few weeks, there are certain things you should ask. Are they licensed? Do they use cognitive behavioral therapy, a short-term approach that helps identify inaccurate thoughts and change behavior?

Hopefully, the therapist or social worker you talk to is beneficial. However, they will not be perfect, and they might not even be helpful. This is very frustrating. If this is the case, remember this is a temporary person who will try to get you through the next day, week, or two. It may also take time to trust the person or feel comfortable with them. Get documentation of your visits in case you need to show this to professors if you miss any classes or assignments.

No matter what type of help you get in the short term, be aware that it is likely temporary; you will need to find a semi-permanent or permanent plan in the future, which is covered in Chapters 6 and 7.

3. Get Back on Track with Your Classes:
Read Each Course Syllabus Very Carefully and Prioritize

You are dealing with depression as a college student. In high school, attendance is mandatory, teachers will notice your absence, alert the administration, and your parents. Attendance is not required in many college classes, so you are likely to fall through the cracks and fail classes. **Be sure to know what is rewarded in each class and put your efforts toward it accordingly.**

Look carefully at the course requirements, the percentage that each part counts toward your grade and when assignments are due. If attendance is required and you missed class, attend the next class as soon as you can and provide the documentation from the health center, so you do not lose the points. For any class you missed, required or not, get a classmate's notes. Rewrite them and make sure you understand the material you missed. (Yes, I know it is much easier to just take photos of them with your phone, but you will not understand the material unless you write it down.)

Spend the most time on the assignments that are the largest part of your grade. Don't spend a lot of time studying for a quiz that only comprises 5% of the class while quickly completing a project that is worth 30% of your grade. **Break your assignments into small, concrete tasks so that it is easier to start and complete what needs to be accomplished.**

If a test is coming up, study as much as you can. Do not worry if you do not do as well as you have in the past. A 70 is much better than a zero if you do not show up to take the test. If you have a paper, do the best you can and turn it in. Again, a D (65) is better than an F (0) and does not bring your grade down nearly as much.

You can still pass a class (or even do fine) with 60s or 70s on assignments. If you get zeros on papers, tests, and projects, you will fail the class.

4. Go Through the Motions for Classes and Everything Else

Have you ever driven your car from one location to another and not remember doing it? It is because you have done it so many times that it is routine, so you don't even think about it. You have already developed a habit of going to class, eating lunch, studying in the library, and other activities. You are depressed and have very low energy. **But continue with your routine as much as you can.**

You have to pretend you are okay, which is not unique; lots of people have to. The difficult part with depression is acting as if you are okay without suppressing your pain. **If you can battle through a depressive day or week, even doing only half of what you typically do, it is still an accomplishment.** It is much better to have five pages of a twenty-page paper complete, than none.

I have days where I feel that there is absolutely no way I can prepare for a class, and then teach it. But I read the textbook (slower), write my notes (sloppier), and do everything else in the same way that I do when I am not depressed. It takes more energy and occasionally my class isn't as good as I would like. But despite my depression, the classes are fine and sometimes very good. *It is so hard*, but I always feel better afterwards.

If you need to, change your routine slightly. When I am really depressed and am walking from my office to class, I take routes where I am unlikely to see anybody. I do not want any interaction with others because I am conserving as much energy as possible for my teaching. When I am not depressed, I socialize with other faculty, staff, and students as I walk to and from class.

Other times when I am just slightly depressed, I purposely walk through areas where I typically see other people I know. The hellos, smiles, and small talk break me out of my funk and give me more energy. **Find what parts of your daily routines can be adjusted to work with your depression.**

5. Push Yourself and Find an Outlet for Your Pain

Fake it until you make it. I tend to be a very pessimistic person and hugely skeptical of the "just do it" mentality. But I find that sometimes playing the part works. Walk across campus and say hi to people you know, get involved with that intramural sport. These brief social interactions can sometimes help pull you out of your low.

Go to the gym, try to exercise. Start running a mile; if you make it, great, if not that is okay too. Your workout is similar to your depression; it is a battle. If you can't do it, try again later. If nothing else, walk around, anything to get your blood moving. Physical activity is not only good for our body but also our mind. Find a green space if possible. Grass, trees, and other outdoor spaces have been shown to positively impact our emotional well-being, including depression. It is a little silly, but the ancient Mayans believed that hugging a tree (literally) would help alleviate melancholy.

Write a poem, draw, sing, paint, or dance. It doesn't matter if you are not good at it. Release your pain with some artistic endeavor. Wander around taking photographs that capture your feelings. Write something, anything. Write about all the bad things in life. Then write about all the good.

6. Do Not Make Any Rash or Big Decisions

Don't get a tattoo, don't join the army, don't buy a motorcycle, don't adopt a dog. And don't quit college. Do not make any major decisions when you are depressed. You may end up with a tattoo, in the military, or riding a motorcycle, but you do not need to do it immediately. Your brain works differently when you are depressed, so your judgment is likely impaired. You have decades ahead of you, so plan out the big choices in life but don't act on them.

7. HOWEVER, Don't Make the $10,000 Mistake: Not Formally Withdrawing

Your goal is to finish college while dealing with depression. **Healing yourself is the most important thing,** *thus, if your depression is so severe that you cannot continue, then dropout temporarily.*

Make sure that you formally withdraw as soon as you have made that decision. It can be difficult to find the steps necessary and the appropriate staff needed to help. In general, you will need to contact the registrar's office, financial aid, and resident hall offices. These bodies are in charge of keeping track of your academic records, monetary obligations, and living arrangements.

If you have an academic or other formal advisor, go to them for help. You do not need to contact your professors, unless you want to send a short email letting them know you will no longer be in class.

If you do not officially withdraw, the school will continue to think that you are still a student even if you are not attending courses or living in a dorm. At the end of the semester, you will have Fs in your classes and still have the student loans to pay back. It can be extremely difficult to withdraw from college retroactively.

In addition, along with the failed classes you may have a grade point average so low that you are dismissed from school for poor academic performance. This will obviously keep you from re-enrolling at your current college and hinder you transferring to another school. The likelihood of graduating from any school in the future is much lower.

Depending on when you withdraw, your classes may not show up on your transcript and you should be reimbursed for part of your tuition. In general, the earlier you withdraw the higher the percentage of tuition that will be refunded. If you leave early in the semester, your classes will not show up on your transcript and it will not hurt your ability to continue in the future.

If you are unable to fill out the necessary paperwork by yourself, have a family member or a friend help. **Make sure that your school knows that you are temporarily stepping out and will continue in the future.** This way you can stay enrolled for classes you have registered for in upcoming semesters if possible. Be sure to know the policy for re-entering your school too. Ask about the process for re-enrolling at the same time you are momentarily leaving.

8. Re-Enter Your Current School (if Necessary)

This is longer term and would obviously only apply if you did leave school. After you have your depression under control, re-enter your college as soon as you can. In some situations, this is straightforward, where you only need to fill out a form. (This is why you needed to formally withdraw temporarily.)

In other situations, there are complicated rules that you must follow to enroll in classes again. You may need documentation from your psychiatrist and family doctor stating that you are stable enough to handle the pressure of college. In some cases, schools require that your leave of absence was "productive." You will need to prove that you didn't just spend months on social media.

In a few instances, you may need to re-apply, so you will go through the same process you did from high school. Unfortunately, some schools have complex rules that make it difficult to return to school if a student has left temporarily. You may need to meet with a school psychologist who will determine if you are prepared to re-enroll. Don't let these obstacles derail your college career. If you truly dislike college, then pursue whatever it is you enjoy.

COPING WITH DEPRESSION IN THE FOLLOWING WEEKS AND MONTHS

I said, Sherman, you can make it through this pain.
You can always find your way through any pain...
This is who I am... I am in pain... And I always find my way home.

~Sherman Alexie
Author[xv]

WHAT YOU DO IN COLLEGE depends on the severity of your depression. After dealing with the immediate onset of it, coping in the following weeks and months entails developing a strategy to complete your classes and find stable treatment. First, get back on track with classes. Second, find semi-permanent professional help and start finding permanent treatment. Third, develop strategies for how else to combat your depression. Fourth, set up a plan to finish the semester.

After that, over the following months, you need to set up a plan for finishing college and preparing for the future. Fifth, be sure to **plan your classes around your depression while also fulfilling college requirements!** Sixth, formalize outlets for your pain. Seventh, be sure to pursue something exciting. Eighth, develop a plan for depression in college (in case it reoccurs). Ninth, evaluate your major, if necessary. And tenth, only if needed, transfer to another school.

1. Get back on track with classes

The same strategies with classes in the short term also pertain here. Focus your efforts on areas that count most for your grade and do as much as possible. **If you are struggling with classes, get help immediately. Email the professor but also go see them directly during their office hours.** If you missed a test or did not turn in a paper or other assignment, see if you can make it up as soon as possible. Be sure to have the form from the health center documenting your missed classes.

If you are doing poorly in a course, you are likely not alone. Responses from professors when you ask for assistance will range from very supportive, to indifference, to animosity. Generally, I would not recommend asking for special treatment or accommodations.[xvi] However, if you politely say you have had some recent difficulties and acknowledge that you are doing poorly but want to improve, most teachers will oblige.

Getting started with catching up on your classes is the hardest part. You may experience anxiety when you return to class and see your professor. However, avoiding this will make you even more anxious. By conquering your fears you become stronger and get back on track. Do it for yourself (intrinsic motivation).

Write a list that breaks course assignments into smaller components. Instead of "write twenty-page paper" make it: 1. review literature, 2. write introduction, 3. list references, etc. This makes tasks less abstract, more concrete, and manageable. After you finish each part, cross it off. This gives you a sense of accomplishment, a kind of high, which helps counterbalance the low of depression.

Find a quiet spot where you can focus on your studies. If you are with friends, it is likely you will get distracted and not be as productive. When studying, shut down your electronic devices so you are not interrupted by texts, tweets, and other social media distractions. If, however, you have a real study group, use it; teaching others helps you learn and helps keep you occupied so that you don't go down the rabbit hole again.

Start each hour or day working on the most difficult class. Then move to the next most challenging course. Finish with your easiest subject. It is easier to move from calculus to reading nineteenth-century English literature than the other way around. If you are unable to focus on the harder material, let it go and work on an easier project first. Whenever you have more energy, go back and work on the more difficult classes and material.

2. Find (semi) permanent professional help and start finding permanent treatment

After experiencing a low period, you may feel fine and think that you don't need help. However, if depression has hit you once, it is likely to hit you again. **The best time to get help is when you feel good** because doing this takes effort.

If the counselor you talked to at the health center was helpful, continue with them as long as possible to get you through the semester and seek out a long-term treatment plan. While working with them, using your parents' insurance, set up a more permanent treatment option outside the school. Depending how far away you live from your family, you may want to consider getting a therapist closer to your college.

If the first therapist you talked to is not helpful, find another one. This can be a frustrating process. You may have someone with a canned solution for you. Other therapists may not truly understand the intricacy of your depression. Or the person may just not be a good match. But the second or the third one could be the right one. Don't mistake a bad experience with one therapist with the process of therapy in general.

As in any profession, there are some who are capable workers and some who are not. Maybe you are more complex than the person you talked to. Nobody will understand 100%, but that's okay, they just need to help with your depression. Use the *Psychology Today* website, https://www.psychologytoday.com/intl, as one source to find a good match.

Ask therapists about the way they approach depression. You are the one in need so make sure you like how they will help you. If you feel at ease talking about everything that is fine. However, if you are embarrassed or ashamed of something, you do not have to share it. Make sure that you are comfortable with who you are talking to. If you want to delve into a difficult topic later, you always have that option. It will take time to develop trust.

Your relationship with your therapist is a partnership so be an active participant. Take notes during your sessions, prepare questions or other topics to talk about in advance. Be sure to do this at your own pace; however, the more proactive you are, the sooner you will feel better and move forward with your life. This will take effort, but as with most things in life, you get out of it what you put in.

Depression is a chemical imbalance, so you may also be referred to a psychiatrist who may try to treat your depression with drugs. Hopefully, this will help, but be aware that there are limitations. It takes weeks or months for them to take effect. They are only effective in about half of the population. But for many people, the drugs can help stabilize them, which then makes therapy even more effective.

There are many different types of selective serotonin reuptake inhibitors (SSRIs) that are used to treat depression. Some work well for certain people but are ineffective for others. The first (or second, or third) drug you take may not help. In addition, there may be significant side effects with them, such as weight gain or an impact on sex drive. If you are pursuing drugs to alleviate your depression, be aware of the difficulties they might have on, not just your personal life, but also your academics. You may want to wait for the summer, when you are not taking classes, to pursue this strategy.[11]

3. Develop other strategies to combat your depression

Find a support network outside your traditional treatment plan. It is possible that on your campus there is already a support group for students suffering from depression. There are also advocacy groups on many college campuses, such as Active Minds Inc. and the JED Foundation, that are reducing the stigma associated with depression. Or join any student organization of your choice. Being around other like-minded students can boost your mood.

Evaluate your social media use. There is a correlation between high use of TikTok, Snapchat, Instagram, and other social media sites and decreased mental health. Online, people might appear cool with a perfect life, which adds to the stress of those suffering from depression. By reducing your time on social media, you might find that not only does your mental health improve, but you will have more time for classes and other activities.

Almost all of us should eat better than we do. Since we do not, at least find those foods that improve your mental health. I have found that raw fish, broccoli, and orange fruits (papaya, cantaloupe) help my mental health. Yes, I prefer eating pizza, and I often do, but making myself eat a little better really does help. I often have a bag of chips or candy bar as a snack. I have been trying to

---

[11] There is a lot of information on treating depression from a large variety of sources including on the Internet, so I do not go into detail on it here.

develop a five-baby carrot and apple habit as replacements. Even eating better occasionally is better than not at all.

Some individuals have found that a Mediterranean diet high in fruits, vegetables, yogurt, legumes, seafood, and whole grains has actually cured their depression when drugs and other treatments failed. At a minimum, eating better will supplement other treatments with no bad side effects.

In addition, not only is there a link between exercise and physical health, but there is also one between exercise and mental health too. There is a large body of evidence showing that regular exercise of as little as 30 minutes, five times a week, improves depressive episodes. Just as all of us have different types of depression, we have different activities that help us.

A short jog by yourself, where you can get engrossed in your own thoughts may be best. You may prefer other solitary activities like light weight workouts or running on a treadmill. Maybe you prefer the companionship of a basketball game where you are focused on the actions of others. Or you may get a lift from the social interaction, in addition to the physical activity, from a game of volleyball.

Tai chi, yoga, and other martial arts exercises are more physically demanding than you may think. In addition, these Eastern practices have the benefit of providing mindfulness, a form of meditation, which has also been shown to decrease depression.

Set aside time each day to recharge your battery. Actions like writing in a journal, listening to music, or other solitary activities may help relax your body and mind. Be sure that they are things that help lift your spirit, not activities that cut you off from other people. Alone time is beneficial for depression, isolation is not.

4. Set up a plan to finish the semester

Evaluate your classes. **With depression, it is inevitable that you will have setbacks; do not let it ruin your academic career.** If you can, complete the semester with the full class load you started with. However, if there is a class that you will fail no matter what, drop it, as long as you maintain full-time student status. If you drop below a certain number of credit hours, you lose your financial aid and other benefits.

Map out the rest of the semester. You are responsible for your work, whether a professor reminds you or not. **Work ahead as much as possible in case a low period hits again**. Start early on papers and other assignments. Block time, weeks, or days in advance, to study for tests, not just the night before. Develop the habit of thinking that class attendance is required even if it is not.

Remember that you must complete all the assignments for your classes. It is the same when I need to prepare for teaching classes, work on committees, lead a seminar, or conduct research for a conference. Since I must focus on these things, it forces my mind to get out of dark places and into productive activities. If you force yourself to do your classwork, your mind is engaged in it. Yes, I realize how difficult this is.

Spend extra time on the beginning of papers. The first few pages set the tone for the rest of it. If you start it well, the professor is more likely to expect the rest of the paper to be good and give you the benefit of the doubt when grading it. Write at least two drafts. Bring your papers to the writing center to be proofread.

Have a classmate, roommate, or someone else check your work. When you are low, you are probably "spacey" and more likely to make simple mistakes. Use the tutoring center to help with your math homework or other difficult classes. If the professor allows it, have them read your preliminary project before turning in the final assignment.

You may end up with Bs or Cs in your classes, not the As you wanted, so you are disappointed because you did not live up to your high standards. Don't dwell on a lower grade than you are used to. Getting good grades, finishing required classes, and graduating on time are important. But right now, the most important thing is to make it through the semester.

Write down reasons to finish college. Money, a job you like, respect from your family, or future endeavors a degree will help with (extrinsic motivation). When I dropped out of college because of my depression, it was because I did not see the point. I wished I had spent a little time reminding myself of the value of a college degree and where I ultimately wanted to go with my life.

5. Plan your classes around your depression while also fulfilling college requirements

For the remaining time you have in college, you need to be proactive. **The next time you register for classes for future semesters, choose some that fit the parts of your depressive personality.** You have many options picking classes to fulfill the typically 120 credit hours required for your degree.[xvii] Generally, one-third of your classes are for your major, one-third are "exploratory" classes, and another third fulfills core curriculum, also called general education (gen ed) classes.

You have some choice, albeit limited, in classes for your major. For some majors like accounting or math, you may not have any choices. For other majors, you have options of taking a class from a list of alternatives. For example, an economics major can take a class on the history of economic thought or feminist economics to fulfill part of that major's requirements.

The purpose of having one-third of the course requirements be exploratory, where students can pick any classes they want, is to try to broaden students' knowledge and make them more well-rounded individuals. Many students use this opportunity to add a second major or minor.

However, if you can literally pick any class available, you obviously can choose classes that you think will help with your depression. Note that these are not classes on or about depression, though there might be one at your school.

Depending on their personality, different people enjoy various types of movies, videos, music, and other entertainment. Some people like superhero movies but hate rom-com ones, whereas others are just the opposite. Some individuals love country music while others are drawn to hip-hop.

There are two important things to do when picking classes. One, if you have not already done so, is to find and take those classes that fit your personality. These are classes that fill college requirements but are less stressful (decreasing the chance of a depressive episode) or may reduce stress because they are so pleasant.

Two, with depression as part of you, there are certain subjects that you will not only comprehend better than others, but you will also enjoy. You are deep and complex and will be able to construe hidden meanings that others are unable to see. Your depression actually helps with reading and interpreting material in some disciplines.

In college, I was a double major in economics and Russian studies, taking about half of my classes in each area in a semester. When I was up, I would study the math and reasoning in my economics classes. I enjoyed the logic associated with this discipline, since there did not seem to be any logic associated with my bouts of depression.

Then during my low periods, I would read about the German invasions of Stalingrad and the suffering of the people and tragic life of Anna Karenina. Russian literature is filled with great writers covering depressing topics in a fascinating manner that those of us experiencing lows understand in a way that others may not.

Read the course catalog (on the school's website or intranet) carefully before registering for classes. Then take classes that you think would be interesting when you are low AND also satisfy degree requirements. Make sure you are aware of all the options you have. Take at least one class you *really* like every semester (preferably more). Today, with information about classes online, it is easy to find classes that appeal to you.

If you have not chosen a major or minor yet, consider one that is general or interdisciplinary. Global studies, environmental studies, Latinx studies, are all broad enough to allow you to mix and match classes from many different areas, culture, arts, political science, and more. Having an eclectic choice of material to study gives you the opportunity to always have something different to focus on depending on how you feel.

The core curriculum (or gen ed) is required for all students. These are mandatory in order to ensure that students know basic math, can write well, communicate effectively, and understand the basics of religion, and science. Within each category, the number of classes has expanded dramatically and there is usually a lot of flexibility to fulfill requirements. Twenty years ago, to fulfill the humanities requirement you would only have a few different literature classes. Now there are classes on movies, music, and video games that fulfill some requirements.

For example, you may be required to take two social science classes that includes economics, anthropology, psychology, history, and sociology. There may be a class in political science on genocide in Cambodia. Yes, this is a very sad and difficult topic, but learning about extremely gloomy topics can put your depression in perspective.

This does not mean you have to change your major or delay graduation. It is a nice change of pace to read about Buddhism that fulfills the religion requirement after studying for your accounting test. Working on a drawing (that fulfills a humanities requirement) may clear your mind after your chemistry class. A course on eighteenth-century Russian writers that explores the miserable living conditions of peasants also fulfills a humanities requirement. A poetry class where you can release some emotions counts as a writing requirement.

When picking classes for upcoming semesters, also mix easier (or different classes) with more difficult ones. When you are up, work on the more challenging classes. And when you are tired of studying finance, you can move to reading nineteenth-century English books. Reading about the sad and lonely childhood of Jane Eyre, her struggles, and finally happy ending is a great diversion for your mind after the logic of supply and demand in economics.

Below is a broad list of categories that possibly work with your depression. In some cases, it may help to take classes that deal with sad topics. Or you may take classes that make you think broadly about life. Perhaps looking at the lighter side of life is best, taking classes on humor. You know yourself better than anyone, so pick what is best for you. Be sure to talk to your academic advisor while picking classes to ensure that you are also fulfilling requirements so you graduate on time.

Though your college may have some of the courses listed, this is a generic compilation of classes across many colleges and universities. If the course description is not clear, check the bookstore for class material to skim through. You may find something you enjoy based on that content rather than the course descriptions. If your bookstore is online, find the tables of contents and sample chapters on Amazon or other websites. Most schools' libraries have a few copies of each book for classes that you can check out for a few hours to help you learn about a potential class. Below are eight broad categories that may help.

A. Active classes

There are opportunities to take courses where you are moving. Obviously, this starts with physical education classes. They can run the gamut from moderately active to very strenuous (weightlifting, tennis). Be aware that there is a limit on the number of credit hours taken in this area that count toward graduation, usually six to eight. And sometimes these classes do not count as part of the core curriculum, so are electives only.

Theater classes provide another way to not just sit in a classroom. While there are obviously parts for actors, there are also many opportunities for setting up the stages, lighting, or otherwise work behind the scenes. In addition to music, there are also often classes in dance or choreography that force you to focus on body movements. Depending upon the nature of the classes, they may or may not count toward the core curriculum so again, pick carefully.

B. Creative classes

The art department not only offers majors and minors but also classes for beginners or those of us who are not naturally artistic. Hands-on classes such as drawing 101 or introduction to pottery may stimulate your brain in a way that combats your depression and likely fulfills a humanities requirement. Classes on photography will help you look at the world around you in a different way or at least help you understand lighting and composition so that you get better pictures for your Instagram account.

There are also many newer classes in this area that are based on twenty-first century technology. There are courses on video arts, using digital technology to take, edit, and create videos. You can use 3-D machines to make your own creations. Or perhaps you want to learn how to develop video games. Peruse your catalog for classes that interest you and fulfill core requirements.

C. "Deep" classes with depressing topics

Since the beginning of civilization, the world has been filled with war, exploitation, economic upheaval, and other sad events. Studying these may fit with some of our depressive moments. .

The Russians have a long list of depressing periods, so classes on the history of Russia are useful to combat some of our melancholic moods. Some specific examples: a class on Soviet films will also count as a humanities class, and a political science class on communist and post-communist systems will fulfill a social science requirement.

Other courses focus on how colonization of certain parts of the world by European countries has led to wars, poverty, and civil strife today. While our depression is awful, there is no doubt that many people suffer horribly while we are more fortunate. This can be explored in twentieth-century Latin American film classes that illustrate how dictators in Central American countries brutalize indigenous populations.

D. Meaning of life

There are some disciplines, such as philosophy and religion that have many classes examining the meaning of life, spirituality, and why evil exists in the world. Of the many topics in this area are classes on existentialism that look at human actions and feelings or Buddhism, in which you will learn that one of the four noble truths is that existence is suffering (and counts as the religion requirement for graduation).

In addition, there are many other authors and books, both fiction and non-fiction, required for classes that cut across many disciplines that also explore this topic. An example includes courses on Fyodor Dostoevsky, who, in part, writes that suffering is a necessary part of life.

Many of these classes will be in the departments of literature or history. They will be on topics such as examining your life through faith, death, and dying; interpreting ancient myths; what is love; where do we (as humans) fit in the world; and contemplating life.

E. Tragedies

There is a long history of literature on tragedies, going back to ancient Greece, through Shakespeare, and continuing to the present. When you read about truly sad situations, it can make you feel that your problems are not that bad in comparison. Your professor will help you unravel the hidden meanings of misfortunes that hit the characters in these stories.

For this area and the next one, there are literally hundreds of options based on the interests and expertise of different professors. These two areas will satisfy either a humanities or social science requirement. Most course catalogs list classes that fulfill these two areas in core (or gen ed), so look online (or on paper) and sort by the requirement. Note that these classes are specialty ones so may not be offered as often as most courses.

F. Light, upbeat subjects

There has been a proliferation of new majors and minors at many schools that offer degrees in American culture or media studies that examine non-traditional areas. This includes courses on films, comic books, current music, and other pop culture subjects. Look for classes on Taylor Swift, Beyoncé, female superheroes, or another topic you are interested in.

G. Improving the world

One goal of every college and university is to help students not only understand the world, but to also teach them ways to improve it. There are many majors in this area with lots of different classes. The most common examine improving the environment, making the world more equal, and using the power of markets to help others.

Majors in environmental studies are the broadest of any discipline encompassing biology, economics, political science, and many other subjects. You can take classes from natural sciences, humanities, or social sciences that explore pollution, such as the emission of carbon, and potential solutions to solve them. There could be a class on climate change that counts toward the science requirement at your university. Classes on ecosystems fulfill the obligatory laboratory science class.

Courses in social justice looks at inequities between groups of people, typically minorities and other marginalized groups, or between developed and developing countries. Whether your background is from one of these groups or not, gaining more insight into it will help you put the world in perspective.

A new area of study, social entrepreneurship, includes classes that show how firms can make money and simultaneously improve society. It is not only helpful to learn about this to gain a better understanding of it theoretically, but also there are enormous opportunities for future jobs in this area. In a future career, you can do well and do good.

H. Gender and ethnic studies

Virginia Woolf and Sylvia Plath are some of the many great female writers. Reading books by them provides a unique insight into life. In addition, many classes in gender studies provide a perspective that helps some of us determine where and how we fit into today's society.

African American studies, Latinx studies, or other ethnic studies may also appeal to you. Learning more about your, or other, cultures may provide insights that help you understand your depression. Blatant discrimination and micro-aggressions have been shown to be detrimental to the mental health of many groups.

As with the tragedies and upbeat subjects' areas, there are lots of options based on the location of schools, their commitment to diversity, and other factors so these are only generic recommendations. Look at the humanities and social science in the core requirements for specific classes at your institution.

Note that this is not an exhaustive list; ask your history, English, philosophy, or other professors about classes. Most teachers really like to talk about their areas of expertise. If they don't know about a certain subject, they may be able to refer you to somebody who does.

6. Formalize outlets for your pain

Find a creative outlet related to your classes, a minor or possibly major. If you can release your inner demons while minoring in music, do it. Do not worry about it not "being practical." It can be extremely important for you. In today's modern, complex economy, many employers like workers with varied interests and different skills. Instead of it harming your future prospects, an art minor may enhance your opportunities with your marketing major.

Even if you can't fit it into your academic career, find a way to express yourself. If you can't escape the pain, accept it, embrace it. Write a blog, draw, anything to channel your bottled-up thoughts and emotions. Instead of letting your mind go to dark places alone or in the social media on your phone, let it feed something creative. It does not have to be a Picasso; it is only for you. Get away from your computer screen and phone and write your thoughts out on paper.

7. Pursue something exciting in the short and long term

There are dozens of interesting things (many of them free) to do in college, so take advantage of them. Go to the Buddhist meditation session. Eat the lunch sponsored by the Latinx Club. Stop by the Guatemalan handicraft exhibit. In the short term, join an organization you have an interest in, play an intramural sport, or go to the local music scene.

Go to a football game, film festival, guest speaker, or other campus event, even if you are not feeling social. When you are depressed, you do not feel like having fun and tend to avoid friends and activities. Socializing sometimes brings you up; if it does not, you are not obligated to stay and can always leave.

Always have something to look forward to. Plan a few activities for the coming months and years. Many students have wonderful experiences with study abroad (or in a domestic city like Washington DC) programs. Plan your academics on living and learning in another country for a semester. It can be intimidating, but new and different experiences are also extremely exciting. Thinking about this adventure may ward off the low feelings you have when depressed. Note that your financial assistance, grants, and other aid can be used for this.

If you don't want to (or can't) spend an entire semester away, engage in a short-term trip abroad. Many colleges offer classes in other countries over the January term, May term or summer. These short-term trips are for just a few weeks. They are led by faculty with expertise on certain countries and often count toward graduation. If your college does not offer these, you can likely take it through another school. Spend three weeks in Europe studying financial crises or a month in Argentina learning Spanish.

Service trips are experiences set up by faculty and/or staff to try to make the world a better place. They are inexpensive (often free), and great way to bond with other students, learn about yourself, and give to society. Your college may collaborate with Habitat for Humanity and you can spend a week in Appalachia building homes. Your campus ministry might travel to Mexico to help paint a school.

Note that **these activities not only help alleviate depression but are also valued by future employers.** Thus, engaging in these actions is good for you in college AND beneficial for your future career, whatever it may be.

At a minimum, take time over the winter or spring break to have a little fun. You can go to one of the traditional spots in Florida or Mexico. Or do something a little different. Go to the mountains to ski, the beach to surf, a prairie to hike and camp. Plan anything exciting that breaks up your typical routine of classes, work, and daily life. Future stimulating activities may help you move through the days when you are struggling.

8. Develop a plan for depression in college

I hope that depression is not part of your future, that you will find a cure. However, for many of us, it is a disease that hits over and over. If your depression reoccurs, you need to be prepared. While it can be devastating, it can also be controlled. Depression won't necessarily limit what you do with your life, but it may constrain how you do it.

First, keep a journal to see if there are any patterns to your depressive episodes. If you know in general when it may potentially hit, you can better prepare for it. Does it only occur during very stressful times of the semester, like finals week? Is it only triggered by traumatic events such as the breakup with a boyfriend? Does it hit certain times of the year like winter when it is bleak, cold, and dreary?

Is depression more likely to hit if you do not have a normal routine? Does it occur after many late-night study sessions but not when you go to bed and wake at the same time? Does your eating and exercise impact the severity of your episodes? It may be that your depression hits you at completely random moments. No matter what, you need to be ready.

Second, develop a habit of working through it. All of us have bad habits, engaging in behavior we shouldn't. Some of us have developed good habits like exercising regularly. A habit is just learned behavior that we do on a regular basis. The hardest part is developing something so that it is part of our routine. **Keeping a routine can be very important in staving off depression.**

Trust me, I know how difficult this is. It may be the hardest thing you ever do in your life. You feel so low that trimming your fingernails feels like climbing Mount Everest. Yet you need to go through the motions. Get in the habit of always going to class, reading the textbook, and writing the paper.

Develop a routine around your low and high periods. When you are feeling fine, go up to the professor after class to ask about the required paper or socialize with classmates. The times you are lower after class, you can just leave for time for yourself to conserve energy.

Third, be organized. **Make lists and keep school projects where they can be easily accessed.** If you need to spend lots of time finding articles you were going to use for a paper, it will make it much harder to write. When students, professors, and staff walk into my office they sometimes comment on how organized I am. They do not know that it is a coping mechanism.

When I am not depressed it is easy for me to remember exactly what I was doing in all my classes, what projects I completed for committees, and where I stopped on my research papers. I can easily remember where electronic files are on my computer and where books I use for different classes are on my shelves. Without thinking about it, when a student wanders into my office, I can immediately find their academic file and help them.

However, when I am low, my brain doesn't work as well so it takes more energy to remember what was where. Being organized makes it easier for me to prepare for classes, complete committee assignments, and other work. It is the same with students with their academic work. If everything is in order, you can move from class to class, making assignments easier.

Fourth, prioritize. Put the most effort where it has the highest payoff. Chances are you are paying a lot of money for college so **make courses your top priority.** You might be working but if you compare the cost of your classes with your wages, you do not want to fail a class, take it again, and pay for it twice.

Fifth, over-prepare whenever you can. When you are depressed, taking tests and writing papers is harder. Get your books as soon as possible and read ahead, do the homework as soon as it is assigned. Start a draft of the paper as soon as possible.

When I am not depressed, I don't need to have everything written down for my lectures, just a few notes reminding me to cover the material. I can think on my feet, easily come up with new examples, answer questions, and make jokes. However, when I am very low, I have much more difficulty with these things. To make sure my classes go well, I over-prepare, having everything written down. If I am up and do not require it, I just use my notes as a guide. But, if I do need it, I am always prepared.

This advice does not mean that depression or college will be easy. I recognize the complexity of your depression. You are way up, a little down, way down, and then in between, all over the map. Nevertheless, while not making it simple, engaging in these actions will make it easier.

Finally, **take time for yourself and figure out who you are.** Depressive episodes can be a time for introspection. When the opportunity appears, take an afternoon or evening off. Put aside all your electronic devices (really) and walk, read, anything to let your mind wander. Think about your strengths, good traits you have, why you are special, and the great things you will do in the next half century.

9. Evaluate your major if necessary

If you are 100% certain that your chosen major is what you want to pursue in the future, obviously stick with it. However, if you are not enjoying the classes in your major or are dreading your future career, then change your area of study to something you enjoy. Hating your classes likely contributes to your depression.

This will be difficult because you will think you wasted your time on the classes you already took. However, even though this may take some additional time and effort, it is much better to switch now than pursue something you dislike for years. You will either have an unfulfilling life or change direction in the future when it is more difficult. There is more information on this in the next chapter.

10. Transfer to another school, only if necessary

Perhaps part, or much, of your depressive episode was caused by attending a college that was not a good fit for you. Maybe the school's size (too big or too small), its culture, certain pressures you feel, or its location did not match your expectations and/or personality. If this is the case, don't drop out of school, but rather transfer to another one (my book, *A Professor's Guide to Success in College*, has more information on picking schools). Be sure that this is the situation; do not use your current school as an excuse for causing your depression if it is not the case.

If you decide to transfer, be sure to figure out exactly what you did not like about the school and ensure that your next one is a good fit. **Transferring to another school will not cure your depression.** I have seen quite a few students think that a different school would be the solution and then they develop an even worse case of depression when they find that this is not the situation after they transferred.

Or you may want to pursue a career that does not require a college degree. If this is the case, follow your true calling. My best friends from high school are auto mechanics and carpenters. I have enormous respect for anybody who works hard and contributes to society. If you are close to finishing, however, you should, since you never know if you may need a degree in the future.

This chapter discussed coping with depression over a time of less than a year. The next chapter provides advice for the following years.

PLAN FOR THE FUTURE

If you are going through hell, keep going.

~Winston Churchill
Former Prime Minister of Great Britain[xviii]

UNLIKE THE PREVIOUS CHAPTERS IN which your strategy for depression in college should generally follow the steps outlined, coping in the following years entails items that, while numbered here, do not necessarily have to be followed in this order. In addition, while they are listed separately, there is a significant overlap between them, particularly on deciding what to study and finding your calling.

1. Change your major if necessary (or get internships or prepare for graduate school)

Some students think that once they declare a major, they are going to work in that one specific career the rest of their life. Others are timid about picking a major because they feel they will be "stuck" in that area forever. Most people change careers (not jobs) at least three times during their life. There are many options for you in the future, so choose something you like now.

You may have entered college picking a major because of a great high school teacher, potential for a good job, or an uncle who works in the field. Sometimes it is something other than having an interest in a particular discipline. After taking a few classes, you may have found that you do not like it *or* have found an area that interests you more. **Don't be afraid to change your mind.** Finding and pursuing what is most interesting to you may not only help with depression but likely will motivate you to work harder and with more passion.

You are young; you have a long productive life in front of you. Step back from your current situation and think about what you really want out of life. It is important that you pick something that fits your strengths, weaknesses, interests, and abilities. What is the most important thing to you? Why? What is the second most important thing? Where do you see yourself in ten years? What are the most important accomplishments you want to achieve? Note that this is coming from a pragmatic professor of management, not a philosopher.

As an undergraduate, I double majored in economics and Russian studies. I thought that my future career would be as an exporter-importer between the United States and what was then the Soviet Union. Thinking I would pursue a career in Russian relations, I even interviewed with the Central Intelligence Agency to work as an analyst. After a typical twenty-two-year-old's experience in the labor market with a few entry level jobs, I decided to go to graduate school. The two big questions were where (close to home or not) and what subject.

After choosing to get a master's degree in economics at the University of Kentucky, I still had to pick an area of concentration. I narrowed it between international and environmental economics, with the previous choice following my initial intended career path. With the latter, I would pursue an area that would help the environment. If I pursued a career in international business, I would have to spend sixty, seventy, or more hours a week working year after year. Though I never said it aloud, in the back of my mind I knew that my depression sometimes took a lot of energy out of me so I would not be able to pursue my initial endeavor. I decided to focus on environmental economics, an area where I could make the world a better place.

2. Find your calling: Looking at potential jobs and careers

For college students (soon to be professionals) suffering from depression it is extremely important to pursue something you are passionate about. If starting your own business and becoming a multimillionaire is your goal—go for it. For others, having a sense of purpose, knowing that you are improving society, and helping others may be important. This gives you hope, even during the low times that feeds your will to get up every day for work and move forward with your life.

This does not mean you have to give up a comfortable life without material possessions. Social work, teaching, and paramedics are some of the obvious career options that lead to a solid middle-class life and benefit society. In addition, there are many other career paths that are not as apparent but pay well and provide a purpose. If you are considering law, there are areas in social justice. If you are interested in business, there are jobs in green energy, clean water, and waste reduction with enormous potential.

Some jobs are so sad and difficult that it takes very special people to do them. I know a woman who has had severe bouts of depression. She is also a pediatric critical care specialist, helping newborn children with life-threatening conditions. This profession provides an outlet for her melancholy while providing a very good paycheck and helps families in very difficult circumstances.

After finishing my master's degree, I moved back to New York City and got a job at a company called Bronx 2000 that was located in a poverty-stricken part of the South Bronx. One of its divisions helped provide low-cost, safe housing that was otherwise unavailable for hard-working individuals in the area. The part I worked for was a recycling company, long before curbside recycling became prevalent in the U.S. When I started, it had a buy-back center where people could bring in aluminum, glass, and other materials, for payment.

The company created jobs for individuals who would have otherwise been unemployed. Homeless people would walk around, picking up garbage that was on the streets, and selling it to us for a little money, while also making the area less of an eyesore. It expanded over the years, creating jobs and diverting material from landfills, thus decreasing our impact on the environment. It was a "do-good" operation that I was proud of, knowing I was making the world a better place. Having a purpose in life was extremely important.

When I decided to change career paths, after working there about four years, I knew I had to continue working in an area that contributed to society. I returned to the University of Kentucky to get a Ph.D. and pursue teaching. In my career as a college professor, I have had a positive, even if small, impact on thousands of young individuals. Sometimes when I am feeling low, I read a few of the nice notes or emails from my former students. The world will be a better place long after I am gone due to the great things these individuals will do.

If I did not suffer from depression and pursued my original dream, would I be a successful international businessperson? Would I be flying around the world in a private jet instead of driving around suburbia in my Mazda 3? Would I have four expensive homes in exotic locations instead of a decent townhouse in a nice neighborhood? I will never know.

I do know with 100% certainty that I am extremely happy with my career choices and where I am today. Though I am far from perfect and need to be a little more patient sometimes, I get enormous satisfaction from my hard work as a college professor. I really enjoy watching young people mature and expand their horizons on their way to adulthood.

When you are thinking about what career or job you want to pursue, start big. Be ambitious, what is your dream job? Do not worry if it is not realistic. What would you like to be remembered for in fifty years when you look back on your life? If this does not work out, follow your second dream. There is not just one dream job available for you, but dozens or hundreds. Focus on areas you think would be fulfilling.

After considering any possibility, look at genuine options available. When thinking about different areas and avenues you can pursue, be realistic about how they fit your personality. Are you self-motivated; if you are given a task, will you complete it without any supervision? Do you need structure? Is a job where you are forced to be in a certain place at a certain time best? Do you prefer a set schedule or is working in a chaotic environment better?

Are you someone who can work hard sixty hours a week for a month or two and then need a few weeks off to relax? Or do you prefer a situation where you can work a solid six to nine hours a day five days in a row, then need the weekend to yourself? Make sure that whatever career path you pursue fits who you are.

Are you an extrovert who likes big crowds and being around people? Or are you an introvert who prefers the company of a few people you are very close to? Do you like animals and want to help them? Would you prefer a job where you can work from home, or do you prefer the social aspects of an office?

Do you do your best work when you are a little afraid? When you take a class that you have to work hard at? Would it be the same for a job? Challenge yourself—what new and different jobs, tasks, and careers would push you forward? There is a high degree of correlation between challenging, meaningful work and an individual's sense of self-worth. Be sure you find what is right for you.

Two important factors in choosing jobs are stress and job security. If high levels of stress cause or exacerbate your depression, obviously look into careers that are less stressful than others. If you like a sense of security, then go into professions such as teaching that offer a high degree of stability.

Look into your potential chosen profession very carefully. **Within most professions there is a wide variability of options.** You might hate corporate accounting but enjoy taxes, both broadly under the same discipline. Google the different types of law you can practice or any other profession. Don't forget to talk to your professors and advisors too.

If your depression only hits when you encounter a bad situation be sure to pick jobs that can accommodate this. These can be personal situations, such as the death of a close relative or things that are completely out of your control such as the outbreak of the pandemic. Do horrible events like this hit you so hard that you need weeks or more to recover? If so, be sure to pick a job that will accommodate this and not a typical 9 to 5 job that requires you to go into the office every day.

If the severity of your depression is extremely bad, there are some companies that are proactive in helping employees with mental illnesses. Starbucks has stated that it would provide free mental health treatments for all its employees.[xix] Other firms such as Prudential Financial and American Express have also recently been more supportive of workers struggling with mental health.[xx]

The Chicago Blackhawks are an example of an organization showing that there may be a lot more possibilities out there than most of us realize. National Hockey League goalie Robin Lehner is a winner of the Masterson Trophy, given to the player who best exemplifies "the qualities of perseverance, sportsmanship and dedication to hockey." When Lehner was a free agent in the summer of 2019, he chose to play for the Blackhawks primarily because they had mental health coaches, including therapists. Lehner has publicly discussed his struggles with bipolar disorder, which he notes entails risks. He stated that "I am not ashamed to say that I am mentally ill, but that does not mean I am mentally weak."[xxi]

However, **err on the side of caution when talking about your mental health with future employers.** In a study by the market research firm Ipsos, almost three-quarters of workers who have depression did not tell their firms that they had it due to their concern that it would negatively impact their job.[xxii] There are laws, such as the Americans with Disabilities Act, that protect workers with mental illness. However, the difficulty of the procedures, the time and effort it takes to use them, makes it prohibitive as protection for most people with depression.

Companies' policies on mental illness, including depression, are extremely varied, and will range from outright resentment to very accommodating. In addition, most people in human resources as well as most managers, are not trained or prepared to handle mental health problems. If possible, before accepting a job find out about the firm's policy. Some companies require that any employee who takes a sick day must provide a doctor's note, so taking a mental health day may not be feasible.

Other firms have policies that allow for personal paid days off for any reason. If an employee is feeling so down that they need a day or week to recharge, time can be taken with no negative repercussions to their careers. Cisco Systems provides workers with "emergency" days off in addition to sick and vacation time that can be used for a mental health day.[xxiii]

The first year or two with an employer is the most important. Some people work hard, impress their boss and other co-workers, and make themselves invaluable. Then they are able to negotiate and make a schedule that works around their depressive episodes.

On a positive note, over the past two decades companies have gotten better at recognizing that mental health is an issue that many of their workers face. Firms are providing more support than they had in the past and will likely do more in the future.

With both the recycling company and the different jobs I've had as a professor, I have had just the right amount of pressure, structure, and freedom. I need to have tasks to complete, glass to sell, trucks to schedule, classes to teach, research papers to write. I am also very self-motivated and do not like constant supervision. So, I do my work within the constraints of my low periods. If I am down on a Friday afternoon, I go and read memoirs to charge my battery, and then go in on the weekends to catch up and get ahead in my work. I know you will find careers that work for you too.

3. Make a (not-quite-a) bucket list (NQABL)

If money were no obstacle, and I know it is, what would you do? Maybe in ten, twenty, or thirty years you'll have the resources to do it. You might be able to do it for less money than you think. Or it will fit into your life in an unexpected way. A romantic trip through Europe with your significant other? Hiking through Patagonia?

Or is it something closer to home? Simple pleasures that help you rejuvenate. Is it being able to spend a worry-free week in a cabin in Wisconsin, spending your days fishing? Do you want to hike the Appalachian Trail for a month? Perhaps your desires include things you want to accomplish personally. Is it learning to play guitar? Being able to cook a fancy French dinner?

You never know what opportunities will appear. Thirty years ago, my not-quite-a bucket list included riding my motorcycle through Mexico, which did not happen. But I was able to be the faculty supervisor for a semester abroad in Costa Rica. I spent fifteen weeks learning Spanish, teaching classes, and traveling around the country. Not the same thing as my original dream, but very similar in that it provided the sense of adventure I needed.

For some of us, having a list of future adventures keeps our mind up when it tends to get low. What happens might not occur exactly how you intended but it will happen in another, and perhaps even better, way. You grow as a person when you get outside your comfort zone.

Or you may be a person who prefers quiet things. You enjoy activities that keep you closer to home or at home. Hobbies you want to practice or spend more time on. Things that divert your mind to a nice place. Toy trains, model airplanes, arts and crafts that make life a little nicer. In this case, plan what would make you comfortable and pursue it.

4. Develop a plan for life that may include depression

For many of us, depression is something that reoccurs throughout our lives, so we need to have a plan. If you did get treatment, you may be taking drugs to help. If you are seeing a therapist, they may support you through difficult times. However, you may still experience depressive bouts. Ultimately, it is up to you to take control.

Do not worry about having future depressive episodes; you will learn to navigate them. I have found that my depression follows a particular rhythm. I am fine for a period of time, and then I hit a low, sometimes very low, period. I do whatever I can to make it through that first difficult time, then after a week or two, I find myself getting better in fits and starts. My mind and body work the same way as my old BMW motorcycle.

When I first try to ride my motorcycle in the spring after the winter, it doesn't start. (My mind and body don't work when I am extremely depressed.) I clean the carburetor and my bike sputters but still won't start. (I go through my routine but still struggle.) Then I pull out the sparkplugs, replace them, and my motorcycle starts and moves but in fits and starts. (I exercise a little and I can function more like normal but not fully.) I change the oil and make some other repairs and my motorcycle runs like new. (I am now in my typical routine and I feel and act fine.) Knowing what to expect helps me.

Keep hope! While there may not be a cure for you now, it is possible there will be in the future. There are now more sophisticated medical techniques that can scan your brain. Scientists are trying to discover biomarkers in us that will better connect drugs and/or therapy to each of our own genetics.[xxiv]

In addition, there are more options for helping you feel better than you know. There are newer, less traditional therapies that may help. Time Perspective Therapy has individuals focus on the present and future, while focusing on the good things in the past. Some people can develop habits so that they focus on the positive aspects of their life that alleviate depression.[12]

I have read thousands of stories about people with depression and the one thing that stands out with **almost all of them is that they say that in coping with depression they need to find time for themselves.** This includes famous celebrities, athletes, lawyers, and economists. It cuts across all types, extroverts, introverts, and people in the public eye and out. If this also pertains to you, be sure to set up time for yourself too. However, **do not isolate yourself from the rest of the world.** There is a big difference between isolation, which can worsen your depression, versus downtime, used to recharge.

If depression is part of your life, you can't deny its existence. You can try but if you really are susceptible, you are only lying to yourself, which will compromise your chances for a fulfilling life. When you accept it, you are on the path to dealing with it. Life is hard and there is no silver bullet for our problems. But life is also wonderful.

---

[12] See the Positive Psychology Center at the University of Pennsylvania for more information.

5. Explore depression: Read books and write down interesting facts

Read books that put your mind in a different place. I enjoy memoirs of people who have battled through depression and still have had successful lives. Reading about others who have similar experiences helps me feel less alone. I give a few examples in the suggested reading at the end of the book.

Read magazines, newspapers, and other real news sources. Write down the parts you see about depression. I find that when I am learning about it, it alleviates some of the depression I feel. In addition, being aware of what is going on in the world helps keep my brain occupied and away from my demons.

Keep exploring and trying new experiences. For example, when I was taking Spanish classes, I learned that the English verb, "to be," has two words, *ser* and *estar*. In general, the word *ser* is used when something is permanent or difficult to change. The sky is blue, my car is small. The word *estar* is used when something can change or is temporary. It is raining, the books are on the desk.

Ser is used to describe peoples' permanent characteristics. He is white, they are tall, el es blanco, ellos son alto. *Estar* is used to describe peoples' temporary characteristics. I am angry, you are sick, estoy enojado, usted esta enferma. *Deprimir(se)* is the verb meaning to get depressed, and *deprimido* is to be depressed. *Estar* is used with *deprimir*, so is a temporary feeling.

6. Tackle the source of your depression (only when ready)

This is something I do not necessarily recommend doing while in college since it can be a very difficult, time-consuming, and painful exercise.

Likely, your genetics predisposed you to depression. And perhaps it was genes and genes only that are responsible. But, depression is also often a function of social and environmental factors. Thus, it could also have been triggered by an event (or multiple events), a bad relationship, or other negative experience in your life. If this is the case, at some point in the future you should try to figure out where your depression comes from.

It could be a traumatic event that you suppressed. Maybe you were bullied in middle school. Or you may be questioning parts of your life such as your religion and you want to leave your church, but you have not yet acknowledged it. It may be struggles with your sexuality.

This is related to, but different from, coping with it in therapy. Confronting the cause(s) of your disease is addressing it directly. This will likely be an extremely difficult process so you need to be prepared for it.[13] For me, it helped to write a book about it.[xxv] In the next chapter, I will describe some individuals with depression. These people have not only overcome their depression, they have also had very successful careers and rewarding lives.

---

[13] I have addressed some of the sources of my depression. When I was thirty-one, I had experiences at work that triggered problems I had as child. I eventually found a good counselor who I was able to talk to about topics I had written about in my diaries but never discussed with another person. While this did not cure my depression, it has helped me understand it better.

YOU ARE IN GOOD COMPANY

You must do things you think you cannot do.

~Eleanor Roosevelt
Former First Lady[xxvi]

WHEN YOU ARE DEPRESSED, YOU often feel as though you are all alone. In a way you are. However, you are also part of a group; you just do not know the other members. I guarantee you have met many people struggling with depression, though you were likely completely unaware of it.

This includes last semester's biology professor, your second cousin, your best friend's second grade teacher, and your dentist. The history department's secretary, your stepmother's brother, the shy woman behind you in your writing class. The quiet person in your dorm at the end of the hall, and your next-door neighbor. You get the idea.

In the fifth century B.C., the ancient Greeks described depression as melancholia: Persistent deep, dark moods that didn't seem to have any basis or reason. Interestingly, they prescribed exercise, diet, massages, and bathing as treatments, things that we know today help. In the Middle Ages, depression was thought to be a disease due to demonic creatures. Depressed women were thought to be witches with the only cure being burned alive.

In the seventeenth century, Thomas Willis began to shed light on the topic, depression's root is in our brains. Treatments in the following years included herbal supplements, music, and opium. By the 1950s, it became clear that depression is a mental illness caused by a chemical imbalance. While we have made progress understanding it, we still have a long way to go. One way for us to cope is to learn about other people's experience with it.

Below I briefly describe some people and then list other **individuals who have succeeded in spite of their depression or thrived because of it.**[14] While many of the people listed are artists (there is a long history of writers, painters, and musicians deriving inspiration from their depression) it also includes others. This list cuts across gender, race, religion, sexual orientation, and other demographic factors.

1. College Student

Kyle Wilson was a relatively typical student who had a severe bout of depression for the first time in college. He had never experienced any mood disorders.[xxvii] He was a good high school student who was recruited to play basketball at the University of Illinois. The stress of college classes, being away from home, and playing a Division I sport triggered anxiety that led to depression. He felt guilty about it because he had so much in life. His *joie de vie* disappeared, he had practically no energy.

He coped by just driving aimlessly through the plains of Illinois. He couldn't concentrate, skipped classes, and then would sleep for hours. One night he drove 12 hours straight home and talked with his parents. His mood disorder was diagnosed, and he recovered.

2. Singer-Songwriter

Demi Lovato started acting at a young age.[xxviii] Her parents divorced when she was very young and she experienced severe bullying while in school. She acted, sang, and danced while growing up despite experiencing depression and other psychological problems.

---

[14] For more information on some well-known people discussing depression see: https://www.youtube.com/watch?v=UJe3tqTUC1Y

Demi is a Grammy award-winning musician with millions of followers on Twitter and other social media sites. She is a strong advocate for mental health awareness, substance abuse, gay and lesbian rights, and other social causes.

3. Comedian

Aparna Nancherla is an Indian American woman, who in addition to doing standup comedy, has been on TV shows.[xxix] She uses her experiences with anxiety and depression as a source for some of her material. She has been successful despite having to overcome obstacles due to her being a woman of color in a field dominated by white males.

Aparna acknowledges that depression has "impeded her productivity and mood but also contributes to her point of view." She has also noted that it can make it hard to go about her day, but she has learned to manage it and work within its constraints.[xxx]

4. Hollywood Actress

Ashley Judd has starred in many movies including *Kiss the Girls* with Morgan Freeman and *A Time to Kill* with Sandra Bullock, Matthew McConaughey, and Samuel L. Jackson. Not satisfied with just her fame as an actress, she also earned a degree from the Harvard Kennedy School. On the surface she seems to have a perfect life, but she has also had her share of low moments.

Knowing that she has had many more opportunities than others have, she has donated her money, time, and fame to many worthwhile causes, improving the world. Her work has helped women's rights, social justice, animal welfare, and more.[xxxi]

5. NBA Basketball Player

The recently deceased Jerry West is still, in some ways, the face of the National Basketball Association, its logo is based on him. He was named one of the best fifty players in the NBA, earning the nickname "Mr. Clutch" while playing under enormous pressure for the Los Angeles Lakers.

His autobiography, aptly titled, *West by West: My Charmed, Tormented Life*, discusses not only his success (and failure) on the basketball court but also his struggles with depression. This shows that even Gold Medal Olympic winners and NBA Hall of Famers face many of the same challenges that the rest of us do.[xxxii]

6. U.S. President

Portraits of Abraham Lincoln show him as a stoic, thoughtful, and serious man. We have learned about his role in the Civil War and the Emancipation Proclamation, but many of us do not know that he also endured many periods of severe depression (at the time called melancholy). His depression did not hinder his abilities to shape our nation, in fact, just the opposite; it helped with his realistic, pragmatic approach to the serious problems the United States faced at the time.

Lincoln believed that through no fault of his own, throughout his life, he suffered more than others did.[xxxiii] He coped by reading, writing poetry, and taking long walks in the woods. During these periods, he also was a successful lawyer, became the leader of the Whig Party in Illinois, was elected to a term in Congress, and later president. **It is impossible to separate Lincoln's depression with other traits of hard work, perseverance, empathy for others, and capacity for deep wisdom.** Historians have claimed that his suffering from depression was a main factor in the development of his other strengths.

7. Civil Rights Leader

Martin Luther King not only pushed for an end to racial inequality but also fought against poverty and war. Most of us are familiar with some of the greatest sermons ever and know about his protests for a better, more egalitarian society. However, as with Lincoln, we are likely unaware that he also suffered from depression. He hints at this in one sermon. "Everybody passionately seeks to be well-adjusted," he said, "...but there are some things in our world to which men of good will must be maladjusted...**Human salvation lies in the hands of the creatively maladjusted.**"[xxxiv]

All of King's traits—creativity, depression, brilliance, and empathy—helped him view the world in a pragmatic, realistic manner that made him one of the greatest leaders ever. His lessons of perseverance, courage, and striving to make the world a better place is something we all should strive for. Individuals with false, unrealistic optimism often cannot see the real magnitude of society's problems.

8. Actor

Dwayne "The Rock" Johnson, is not someone the public would consider weak by any means. Yet he and his family have struggled with depression. Here are a few quotes from an interview with U.K.'s *Express* that we would not expect from him. "Struggle and pain is real. I was devastated and depressed. I reached a point where I didn't want to do a thing or go anywhere. I was crying constantly. It took me a long time to realize it but the key is to not be afraid to open up. Especially us dudes have a tendency to keep it in. You're not alone."[xxxv]

9. Musician

Mariah Carey has described her depressive episodes as having very low energy. At first she thought she just had a severe sleep disorder. But in 2001, she was diagnosed with bipolar disorder (also known as manic depression characterized by extreme mood swings from ups/mania to downs/depression.[15] After years of suffering in silence she opened up about it and says, "I refuse to allow it to define me or control me."[xxxvi]

Below is a list of other people, in no particular order, who have also coped with depression. If you Google it, I am sure you will find many, many more.

- Terry Bradshaw, TV commentator and NFL Hall of Fame football player

- Dorothy Hamill, winter Olympic gold medalist

- Bruce Springsteen, musician

- Ricky Williams, college football hall of fame running back

- Chamique Holdsclaw, WNBA women's basketball player

- Eric Clapton, musician

- Trevor Noah, late-night talk show host

- Winston Churchill, prime minister of the United Kingdom

- Amanda Beard Summer, Olympic gold medalist

- Wil Wheaton, actor

- Rachel Bloom, comedian

- Gandhi, leader of the Indian independence movement

---

[15] National Institute of Mental Health

In addition, there are human rights lawyers, astronauts, economists, and individuals from every other profession. There are literally millions of people who struggle with depression with very successful lives. **If these individuals can succeed, so can you!** I realize that most of them are much older than you. There are many young people who will join this list, they just have not had time yet to succeed and tell their stories. You may be one of them.

There is a high correlation between depression and certain personality traits. People tend to be complex. Life is easier for simple people who see the world in black and white. You have deep thoughts that other individuals do not have. This is difficult, but **your complexity is part of what makes you interesting.**

You are insightful. You likely see variations in a topic that other people view as right or wrong. You are good at problem-solving. You are intelligent. Your brain works more than most others. You may be very creative. Don't just focus on the negative sides of depression; there are parts of it in you that will help you succeed in the future.

Ironically, people with depression (not just comedians) often have a good sense of humor. The depressiveness in us makes more empathetic and fosters a sense of realism that allows us to correctly assess situations in business, law, medicine, and other professions. We also tend to listen to other people more, which provides us with different, broader perspectives.

Be sure to figure out your traits and how they fit in the world that helps you navigate it. Sometimes I prepare for the worst-case scenario. This is a pessimistic approach to life, not a negative one. When I send an academic article out for potentially being published, I work hard to make it as good as I can. But I prepare myself for it to be rejected and if it is accepted, I get a high that combats my depressive personality.

Depression sometimes makes us forget about why we are doing certain important things, including finishing college. Thus, in the next chapter, I provide some simple reasons to stay in college and get your degree.

9

YOU CAN MAKE IT

The privilege of a lifetime is to become who you truly are.

~Carl Jung
Psychologist[xxxvii]

DEPRESSION CAN MAKE YOU SCARED to try something new. I was afraid to write this book, fearful that my depression would keep me from completing it. I obviously overcame my fear. While writing this, I led a productive life. I taught hundreds of students, mentored dozens of others, supervised student's independent research and internships. I published original journal articles, developed a new major, taught new courses, and engaged in many other professional activities.

I also drove my daughter to softball practice, watched my son lose many basketball games, and traveled with students, my family, and by myself. While part of me is someone who suffers from depression, it is far from being all of me. I am a successful professional, good friend, and caring father. I am a world traveler, part-time writer, amateur photographer, slow runner, and mediocre cook. Too many people just identify as one or two things and lead incomplete lives. That is not you!

Though you are someone who suffers from depression, it is only part of you. You are a DJ for the radio station, D III cross-country runner, president of the Finance Club, vice president of the Read a Book Club, treasurer of the Student Government Association, or a residence hall director.

Take advantage of college to help you determine your identity and chart your path to success. Below I provide some excerpts from another book of mine, *A Professor's Guide to Success in College*, to provide reasons for completing your college degree. The suggestions are relevant for all college students but can also be a reminder to those struggling with depression, of why you should get your degree.

1. Reasons to Stay in College

Colleges are full of interesting, smart, vibrant young adults. **It is a great place to meet people with similar and different interests.** You have the option of attending events, joining clubs, trading ideas about movies and sports.

College prepares you for change. Doing different things, exposing yourself to new activities, helps you learn how to deal with change. In today's rapidly fluctuating world, it is not only what you know but also how quickly you adapt to varying circumstances. College helps teach you how to learn.

College is a great time to grow as an individual, to become an adult, a great way to grow into yourself as a person. There are few occasions where you get the opportunity to find out so much about yourself.

If a student is looking for an excuse to drop out of college, including having depression, they will find one. Sometimes we get so focused on the negatives that we forget about the positive aspects of something. This certainly can happen in college. In the middle of a semester, it is easy to get bogged down in the mundane aspects of reading textbooks and studying for tests. Some students lose track of the big picture.

The ability to persevere through challenges and difficult situations is tough for most of us. **Getting through college one semester at a time shows perseverance.** It is concrete; the registrar's office has a record showing that you have completed a certain number of credit hours toward graduation. **These accomplishments build confidence.** If you learn how to persist in college, you will be better able to persevere in other areas later in life.

College gives you the opportunity to work on life skills and people skills. There are different types of intelligence: book smart, street smart, common sense, emotional intelligence. College gives you the opportunity to work on all of these. It also helps you work on time management; it helps develop intellectual curiosity and otherwise provides venues to improve yourself. It also helps develop or improve work habits.

We all want to belong, be important or part of something; at college you can be somebody special. You can be a radio disc jockey, the captain of the debate team, the president of the student accounting society, or a leader of innumerable other organizations. You can explore different things; learn who you are and why you are unique.

2. Reasons to Finish College

Once you finish, a college degree is something that can never be taken away. It is an accomplishment, a statement of identity. One of the best reasons to finish college is the doors it opens. A college degree gives you alternatives. You may want to spend your life working at something that does not require a college degree, which is great. But it is better to choose that profession and have alternatives than not have any other choices.

Your mom cares, a therapist will listen, and dad will help. But it is up to you. Accept who you are and do the best you can with what you have. **Despite depression, you will make an impact on this world. You are stronger than you think.** Keep going to find out just how strong. You can still create, travel, make, explore, and do great things.

SUICIDE

If you are going through that dark period, go to your family
and closest friends. Don't put yourself in danger.
It's very crucial that you get your feelings out—
but don't ever inflict harm on your own body.

~Demi Lovato[xxxviii]

I WAS AFRAID TO WRITE this part, but felt I had to. Some people might think that if depression occurs repeatedly, then life is not worth living. My academic career is based on logic, reason, and facts. Research has shown that talking about suicide decreases the risk of attempting it and not talking about it increases the risk. Thus, following the advice of experts I included this chapter.

We also need to be aware that suicide rates have gone up significantly over the past decade. It is the second leading cause of death among ten- to twenty-four-year-olds. A recent survey showed that 25.5% of eighteen- to twenty-four-year-olds have considered suicide.[xxxix] If this is you, call 988 for the National Suicide and Crisis Lifeline https://988lifeline.org/. Or text HOME to 741741 to connect with a volunteer crisis counselor.

People with chronic depression are more likely to attempt suicide than those with acute forms because they have been suffering longer. Other signs of suicide include withdrawing from typical activities, alterations in sleep, spending more time at home, an increase in the use of negative words in social media posts, and other changes in behavior. Attempted suicide rates are higher during the school year and after a famous person commits it.

I was driving to work one day and there were two women on the radio talking about people jumping off a bridge to commit suicide. "They must be crazy," one said. "There must be something wrong," said the second. I thought to myself, yes to number two but absolutely not to number one.

Unfortunately, life is harder for some of us than it is for others. Phrases such as "the Lord never gives you more than you can handle" is not true for everybody. Anybody who has thought about, attempted, or committed suicide has been given more than they can handle.

People who cut themselves, take drugs to extremes, engage in risky sex, and many other destructive behaviors have been given more than they can handle. They need an outlet to deal with the extra burdens of life.

I am not 100% certain, but I am 98% sure that I've felt close to suicide a couple of times in my life. (When I was in college was not one of them.) When I was in my twenties, when I was low, I would get on my motorcycle and get it up to speeds of 100 miles per hour, barely keeping it on the road. Looking back, I'm not sure if that was suicidal or just stupid. It was one example where I have engaged in behavior to mask my pain. I go through periods where I drink too much to numb the pain. There have been times when I wander through very dangerous areas in cities as a coping mechanism.

Over a decade ago in Manuel Antonio, Costa Rica, on a beautiful beach, with perfect water, and a spectacular sunset, I swam out ten, twenty, then thirty minutes away from the shore, far beyond any distance I had swum before. I wondered what it would be like if I kept going until I couldn't anymore.

One thing is for certain. I did not ever feel that the world would be better without me, just the opposite. It is the same with you; the world is a better place with you in it. Sometimes it may feel as though you are not 100% you. But moving at half or three-quarters speed in life is okay occasionally. Go and keep going. Do and show the great things you will do for yourself, and everybody else.

AFTERWORD: COVID-19

Si se puede (If you can).

~Jeison Aristizabal[xl]

THE PANDEMIC WAS ABSOLUTELY HORRIFIC in terms of health problems, lives lost, and social isolation. Though certain problems have persisted, currently we are in a "new normal" in higher education. While it is slightly transformed, most colleges are back to having mostly in-person classes, sporting events, student group meetings, and other typical college activities. I personally believe that the pandemic has made many of us realize how important all the social aspects of college are and will lead to even more of them in the future. Most of us (including introverts like me) are social creatures that need personal interactions that we can't get from our screens.

Nonetheless, there is no doubt that Covid-19 has impacted all of us, and likely those of us with depression even more. If Covid-19 seriously affected your emotional well-being, look at exactly how it impacted you. Did it make you more nervous, apprehensive, fearful of the future, and concerned about job prospects? Below are some things you may have experienced and how you can use the current situation to better prepare for the future.[16]

Due to the stay-at-home requirements did you hibernate more than usual, isolating yourself from others? (I did.) If so, if you have not yet, get out to meet other people through clubs, sports, or volunteering. See if you can make

---

[16] If you have experienced severe anxiety, uncontrollable crying, or other psychological problems, make sure to work with a psychiatrist or other qualified professional to help.

connections so that you have a social network that can support you when get low.

Did the economic disruption from the pandemic make you scared about future job prospects? If so, investigate careers that are relatively recession-proof. Look at the areas that did not have significant reductions in employment. The Bureau of Labor Statistics (https://www.bls.gov/) has information on jobs, industries, and how they have been impacted.

In addition, you can look at social trends. It is very difficult to predict exactly what jobs will be available in a decade or two. Thus, if you are looking for a career with job security look at broad demographic, cultural, and economic trends. Factors such as climate disruption, artificial intelligence (AI), increasing income inequality, and heightened political tensions pose significant challenges. However, they also provide many job opportunities for people who see the effects they will have.

Climate disruption has caused weather extremes that has led to more droughts, fires, and other problems that damage homes. The insurance industry will need employees who be able to better quantify and predict events. A person with a depressive personality is at an advantage because they are generally more pragmatic and realistic than other people.

There will be certain industries that will exist no matter what happens in the future in solid waste, energy, water, and technology. Some jobs related to energy are very cyclical, such as oil drilling. Others though, such as jobs in energy transmission, will exist no matter what occurs. Note that it does not matter if the energy is from fossil fuels, solar, or wind, we need to get it from the source to our homes. Clean water is another industry that will never disappear.[17]

If your chosen future career is something that is potentially unstable, such as in the arts, but you love it with a passion, follow it. But consider taking up a hobby, perhaps one that can provide extra income that you can fall back on if something temporarily happens to your job.

Facing this crisis, perhaps you are one of those people who responded by volunteering to help at a food bank or other non-profit organization. Helping

---

[17] I grew up relatively poor, so up to very recently, have always been concerned about money. Thus, when I picked careers and jobs, I chose ones that had a high degree of security. When I took the job with a recycling center some of my friends and family were concerned that recycling was just a trend. I said that may be, but consumption and solid waste would not go away.

others provides a sense of self-worth and gives you optimism for how you can make the world better. Think about what you like and follow it. There are careers in areas of poverty, health, racism, and sexism, among many others that will always exist.[18]

Hopefully the worst effects of Covid-19 are in the past and we are better prepared if something similar happens in the future. The best we can do, both those of us who suffer from depression, and those who do not, is to take the horrible experience and try to learn a little more about ourselves.

---

[18] There is more information on "do good" jobs in Chapter 7.

SUGGESTED READING

Physical pain tells you that you are alive.
Mental pain challenges your ability to stay that way.

~NPR
January 23, 2015

WHEN I HIT MY LOWEST of lows, I am 100% certain that nobody in the history of the world has ever felt worse. Which is not to say that this is necessarily untrue, but reading other people's account with their struggles or information about it helps me put it into perspective.

Darkness Visible: A Memoir of Madness by William Styron describes his horrible depression in a very clear and succinct book. Note that you may have similar feelings and experiences with some of what is written and nothing in common with other parts.

Prozac Nation by Elizabeth Wurtzel is extremely self-centered and narcissistic but does a good job explaining the pain of depression that those who have not experienced it don't understand. Though it is old, it is written from the perspective of a child and young adult so it may be helpful to most college-aged students.

How Sadness Survived: The Evolutionary Basis of Depression by Paul Keedwell is a multi-disciplinary book on depression. It looks at the history of the disease, why it is so prevalent, and how depression may actually provide benefits to those suffering from it.

A First-Rate Madness: Uncovering the Links Between Leadership and Mental Illness by Nassir Ghaemi is an interesting look at how "sane" people lead as compared to those with depression and other mental illnesses.

The Noonday Demon by Andrew Solomon goes into great detail about practically every aspect of depression.

Other memoirs about struggles that are overcome are: *Wild* by Cheryl Strayed, *All That Is Bitter and Sweet*, by Ashley Judd, *In the Water They Can't See You Cry* by Amanda Beard, and *An Unquiet Mind* by Kay Redfield Jamison.

QUIZ

Since I am a college professor, this book needs to end with a quiz.

1. **What parts of this book were written when I was very depressed?**

   a. Chapters 1 and 5

   b. Chapters 2 and 3

   c. Chapters 4 and 6

   d. None of the above

   e. All of the above

2. **What parts of this book were written when I was slightly depressed?**

   a. Chapters 1 and 5

   b. Chapters 2 and 3

   c. Chapters 4 and 6

   d. None of the above

   e. All of the above

3. **What parts of this book were written when I was not depressed at all?**

   a. Chapters 1 and 5

   b. Chapters 2 and 3

   c. Chapters 4 and 6

   d. None of the above

   e. All of the above

Answer:
I do not have any recollection at all.
This is just a silly way to illustrate that you can accomplish many things while coping with depression.

EPILOGUE

IN MY SECOND YEAR OF college, 1984, I got really depressed. I was a typical nineteen-year-old, I had a great group of friends that I would play racquetball and listen to music with. I tried to talk to some of them about the pain. They made light of it. If I wasn't going to be "one of the guys" they didn't want to be with me. In hindsight, this makes perfect sense; they were not prepared or capable of helping.

Prior to this, there were other situations where some other guys tried to talk to me about their feelings and problems. I forget how, but I basically told them I wasn't there for them either. Maybe it should have occurred to me, but it didn't, that most friends are not capable of helping with some things. Depression for many of us is one of them. I dropped out of school, not knowing where to turn for help. Maybe there was a counseling center or other place where I could get support, but it didn't even occur to me to look for it.

Fortunately, this has changed. Younger people are more open-minded in many ways, including being more open to acknowledging differences and limitations in all of us. However, just be aware that for some of you there might not be support from friends or family.

I returned to college and got my degree. Even with depressive episodes over the past four decades, I have managed to have a successful life. Below are some parts of my journal over time that illustrate some of the down periods. So, if, and/or when, the depressive episodes hit you, I hope that this provides a little comfort knowing that you are not alone and that you can get through it too.

February 1987:

As some people are physically handicapped, sometimes I feel mentally handicapped with depression making me unable to move, unable to function.

April 1988:

Right now, I feel if one can overcome these feelings of depression and despair it makes one a stronger person and more resilient to the world.

August 1988:

My old companion has caught up with me again. It's not a person or object. Nope, it's an unwelcome friend who invades my inner soul.

December 1989:

When I get depressed, I get very quiet. I don't like to talk and would just as soon be all by myself.

May 1990:

I now have a "controlled" depression. I can stay high/up enough at work to manage my way through a day or week. Then I can take my "low" feeling out when I'm by myself after work or on a weekend. I could never control my depression before, in many ways it is a survival tool.

August 1990:

You don't stop getting depressed as you age. But you do learn how to deal with it better. You learn to realize that while it is horrible, it will go away. You learn that things may not be quite as bad as they seem. You can understand and work with or around your depression until it passes. And it always does pass.

October 1991:

I still get low, I still get depressed. But as I get older, as I mature, I learn to accept these feelings rather than fight against them. No matter what happens I will be all right.

It is important to note that there were lots of periods of many months to even years when I did not experience depression.

Fast-forward a couple of decades.

March 2018:

I applied for the faculty supervisor position in Costa Rica for the fall term (and was accepted). Typically, when I have an adventure coming up, I am excited. But I felt nothing because I was depressed. Even though I felt low, I knew I should apply because when the depression lifts, I will be excited. (A month later. Yep. Really excited.)

August 2018:

Yesterday I could not type one sentence I was so low. Today I feel fine and am making great progress on this book.

November 2018:

Monday of week 12 in my semester in Costa Rica. Alarm went off at 6:30; I have a cold and did not sleep well. I am very tired after three months of teaching, taking Spanish, helping students with their struggles, and dealing with problem students. I am on the verge of depression. I could just lie in bed all day, I have no classes, meetings, or other obligations. Nobody would know. I force myself out of bed, go through my routine, and struggle to go for a run. I trudge along, then as I slowly run up a hill, an old man steps aside so that I can pass him, I give him a friendly nod of thanks and mumble "gracias." This gives me a little boost. Later I am sitting on a full bus when it stops. An elderly lady and her daughter get on. I get up and give my seat to the old woman. The daughter smiles at me and says, "muy amable." This is a thank you for being polite phrase and this gives me a little more energy. I am now making progress on this book. I could have let depression settle in, but I didn't. I went home a little early but still accomplished work on this book.

May 15, 2023:

The semester is over, and I move from teaching to research. Forced myself to go to the gym and had an okay workout. I did not want to do anything (and I didn't have to). But started the second edition of this book. I felt better having accomplished something.

June 5, 2024:

I feel so low, but forced myself to work on the edits. Only managed to work two hours but felt better afterwards, as I always do.

ENDNOTES

PREFACE
[i] The epilogue contains a few notes I have written over the decades about my struggles with depression. I know it is self-centered, but I hope that by reading it you will see some of it in you that hopefully makes you feel less alone in your journey.

INTRODUCTION
[ii] *Washington Post*, June 4, 2014.

[iii] *Chronicle of Higher Education*, July 19, 2019, p. A20.

[iv] *New York Times*, October 16, 2023, Ellen Barry

[v] https://www.mayoclinichealthsystem.org/hometown-health/speaking-of-health/college-students-and-depression

CHAPTER 1
[vi] *Chicago Tribune*, Nov. 14, 2004, Kyle Wilson Average college basketball player.

CHAPTER 2
[vii] CBSNews, Oct. 14, 2007.

CHAPTER 3
[viii] *New York Times*, Feb. 27, 2012.

CHAPTER 4
[ix] YouTube video.

[x] *The Healthy Minds Study*, 2018-2019, Data Report, University of Michigan.

[xi] College Students Anxiety, Depression Higher Than Ever but So Are Efforts to Receive Care, Heinze, Justin https://sph.umich.edu/news/2023posts/college-students-anxiety-depression-higher-than-ever-but-so-are-efforts-to-receive-care.html

[xii] There are some organizations that are trying to lessen the stigma, but they are not as well-known or funded as other organizations for other health issues.

[xiii] *People* magazine, Dec 18, 2006, p. 110.

CHAPTER 5
[xiv] *San Francisco Chronicle*, May 20, 2003.

CHAPTER 6

[xv] *You Don't Have To Say You Love Me*, Sherman Alexie, 2017, p. 277.

[xvi] This is different from accommodations for learning disabilities where you need extra time to take tests.

[xvii] There are some exceptions to this such as degrees in engineering and other professional areas and some schools require slightly more.

CHAPTER 7

[xviii] This quote has been attributed to Winston Churchill but there is not a formal reference to when he said it.

[xix] *Wall Street Journal*, March 17, 2020, Patrick Thomas.

[xx] *Wall Street Journal*, August 16, 2017, Francesca Montana.

[xxi] *Chicago Tribune*, July 28, 2019, Jimmy Greenfield.

[xxii] *Wall Street Journal*, August 16, 2017, Francesca Montana.

[xxiii] *Bloomberg Business Week*, November 18, 2019.

[xxiv] *Wall Street Journal*, June 25, 2013, Andrea Petersen.

[xxv] It is *Broken Plates and Old Forests, Navigating Childhood Age 8 to 16.*

CHAPTER 8

[xxvi] https://brightdrops.com/eleanor-roosevelt-quotes.

[xxvii] *Chicago Tribune*, Nov 14, 2004.

[xxviii] https://en.wikipedia.org/wiki/Demi_Lovato.

[xxix] https://www.vice.com/en_us/article/7xzvbb/comedian-aparna-nancherla-on-having-compassion-in-the-face-of-bigotry .

[xxx] https://www.vulture.com/2016/03/depression-and-comedy-with-aparna-nancherla.html.

[xxxi] Ashley Judd and Nicholas Kristof, *All That Is Bitter and Sweet*, 2001, Ballantine Books.

[xxxii] Jerry West and Jonathan Coleman, *West by West*, 2011, Little, Brown and Company.

[xxxiii] *The Atlantic*, Lincoln's Great Depression, Joshua Wolf Shenk, Oct., 2005.

[xxxiv] https://www.psychologytoday.com/us/blog/mood-swings/201201/martin-luther-king-depressed-and-creatively-maladjusted.

[xxxv] *Chicago Tribune*, April 3, 2018.

[xxxvi] *Chicago Tribune*, April 12, 2018.

CHAPTER 9

[xxxvii] https://www.goodreads.com/quotes/75948-the-privilege-of-a-lifetime-is-to-become-who-you.

AFTERWORD: SUICIDE

[xxxviii] *Seventeen*, Apr 12, 2011.

[xxxix] Center for Disease Control and Prevention.

COVID-19

[xl] CNN Interview.

ACKNOWLEDGMENTS

Thanks to everybody at Windy City Publishers.

Special thanks to Chris Nelson, Melanie Zimmerman,
and Ellen DeBerge for their editorial help that greatly improved this book.

ABOUT THE AUTHOR

AFTER GRADUATING FROM THE STATE UNIVERSITY of New York at Albany (SUNY), Jeff worked in the private sector for a few years. This included short stints at a large company, group homes for disadvantaged individuals, a non-profit, and as an adjunct professor at a community college. He then returned to school and taught classes at the University of Kentucky where he got his PhD in economics.

He taught classes in Public Policy at New Jersey Institute of Technology (NJIT) for three years, then spent another three years as a professor of environmental economics at the University of Wisconsin at Whitewater (UWW). He has been at North Central College (NCC) for the past two decades. He currently teaches classes on quantitative business and environmental issues.

Dr. Anstine is considered an "expert" in a few areas because of his PhD, teaching, and research. Depression is not one of those areas. However, this does not mean he is not qualified to write this book; just the opposite. Economists study income inequality and poverty, typically using numbers and data. Individuals who have grown up poor certainly have knowledge, information, and insight that the well-to-do PhD economists do not. The same holds with the surgeon who treated Jeff's cancer. He is an expert but does not know other things about the pain that those who have experienced it do.

There are also individuals who have struggled with depression and then gone on to spend their lives helping others with it. This is fine too, but Jeff believes his perspective as someone whose jobs and careers are focused on the broader issues in business and academia provides a different and pragmatic view that is also helpful.

This is Jeff's third book. His first book is titled *A Professor's Guide to Success in College*, and his second book, *Broken Plates & Old Forests*, is a memoir about his difficult childhood.